Praise for Eddie Bravo & The Rul

*"Eddie Bravo is more than a Brazilian Jiu-Jitsu Black L
creator, an innovator, and a craftsman to a new style of grappling that is
transforming everyday guys into submission machines. Instead of playing the wait game for your opponent to make a mistake, Eddie pushes the
envelope and forces his opponents into MAKING mistakes. Eddie Bravo's
style is subtle, but explosive, flowing from one limb-trapping submission to
another. Buy Eddie's book, read the book, and start putting his techniques
to work—because if you don't, you will soon be tapping out to some guy
who did."*

**'Big' John McCarthy
UFC Referee**

*"Eddie Bravo has accomplished something very rare in jiu-jitsu, especially
among Americans. He has developed a unique series of positions—his
'Rubber Guard'—and successfully utilized these positions at a high level
of competition."*

**Ricardo Liborio
Brazilian Jiu-Jitsu Legend**

*"Eddie Bravo's approach to jiu-jitsu is so unusual and innovative that it's
literally a completely separate branch off the jiu-jitsu tree. And it's not just
different; it's actually better. Much better."*

**Joe Rogan
UFC Commentator
Host of NBC's 'Fear Factor'**

*"We were the first to shock the world with Eddie's skills on our site years
ago. Ever since then we knew he was going to branch out and change the
game with style. Eddie Bravo is All-American jiu-jitsu."*

**Scott Nelson
Onthemat.com**

Books By Victory Belt

Mastering the Twister by Eddie Bravo with Erich Krauss & Glen Cordoza

Guerrilla Jiu-Jitsu: Revolutionizing Brazilian Jiu-Jitsu by Dave Camarillo with Erich Krauss

Mixed Martial Arts: The Book of Knowledge by BJ Penn with Erich Krauss & Glen Cordoza

Grappling (vol. 1): The Book of Knowledge by BJ Penn with Erich Krauss & Glen Cordoza

Grappling (vol. 2): The Book of Knowledge by BJ Penn with Erich Krauss & Glen Cordoza

Grappling (vol 3.): The Book of Knowledge by BJ Penn with Erich Krauss & Glen Cordoza

Brazilian Jiu-Jitsu (vol.1): The Book of Knowledge by BJ Penn with Erich Krauss & Glen Cordoza

Brazilian Jiu-Jitsu (vol.2): The Book of Knowledge by BJ Penn with Erich Krauss & Glen Cordoza

Brazilian Jiu-Jitsu (vol.3): The Book of Knowledge by BJ Penn with Erich Krauss & Glen Cordoza

Projects by Eddie Bravo

Mastering the Twister (book) by Eddie Bravo with Erich Krauss & Glen Cordoza

10th Planet Jiu-Jitsu: Mastering the Rubber Guard (DVD) by Eddie Bravo

The Twister (career highlight DVD) by Eddie Bravo

compella and the twister (music CD)

Eddie Bravo's Projects Available at www.THETWISTER.tv and www.VICTORYBELT.com

Books by Erich Krauss

Muay Thai Unleashed by Erich Krauss & Glen Cordoza

Beyond the Lion's Den by Ken Shamrock with Erich Krauss

Jiu-Jitsu Unleashed by Eddie Bravo with Erich Krauss

Brawl: A Behind-the-Scenes-Look at Mixed Martial Arts Competition
by Erich Krauss & Bret Aita

Little Evil: One Ultimate Fighter's Rise to the Top by Jens Pulver with Erich Krauss

Warriors of the Ultimate Fighting Championship by Erich Krauss

Wall of Flame: The Heroic Battle to Save Southern California by Erich Krauss

Wave of Destruction: The History of Four Families and History's
Deadliest Tsunami by Erich Krauss

On the Line: Inside the US Border Patrol by Erich Krauss & Alex Pacheco

10TH PLANET JIU JITSU

MASTERING THE RUBBER GUARD

Jiu-Jitsu for Mixed Martial Arts Competition

Eddie Bravo

with Erich Krauss & Glen Cordoza

Photography by Eric Hendrikx

Victory Belt Publishing

California

www.VICTORYBELT.com

RUBBER GUARD

HALF GUARD

-The Lockdown (pg. 54)
-The Jaws of Life (pg. 56)
-The Whip Up (pg. 58)
-Old School (pg. 60)
-Electric Chair Sweep (pg.63)
-Electric Chair Submission (pg. 63)
-Stoner Control (pg. 66)
-Stoner Control Variation (pg. 68)
-Stoner Control Arm Triangle (pg. 70)
-Stoner Control Calf Crank (pg. 70)
-Twist Back & Plan B Combo (pg. 71)
-Half Guard to Closed Guard (pg. 73)

FAILED DOUBLE UNDER-HOOKS
-The Stomp (pg. 92)
-The Super Stomp (pg. 94)
-The New Stomp (pg. 96)
-The Godfather (to Full Guard) (pg. 98)
-The Godfather Sweep
 to Side Control (pg. 100)

FORCING THE LOCKDOWN
-The Stakeout (pg. 102)
-Butt Scoot Blast (pg. 104)

BUTTERFLY GUARD

-Jean Jacques Sweep (pg. 110)
-Stick Shift (pg. 112)
-Jean Jacques 2 (pg. 115)
-Cocoon to X-Guard Sweep (pg. 117)
-Cocoon to Dogfight (pg. 121)
-Cocoon to Pyramid (pg. 122)

HALF GUARD DOGFIGHT

-Transition into the Dogfight (pg. 75)
-Half and Half (pg. 76)
-Half and Half Variation (pg. 78)
-Plan B (pg. 80)
-Twist Back & Plan B Combo (pg. 71)
-The Powder Keg (pg. 84)
-D.P.O to Side Control (pg. 85)
-D.P.O to Back (pg. 87)
-Drowning Wizard (pg. 89)

CRACK HEAD CONTROL

The Pump (pg. 150)

PYRAMID

-Triangle (push hand out) (pg. 157)
-Triangle (pushing hand up) (pg. 158)
-Tepee (pg. 159)
-Go-Go Plata to Loco Plata (pg. 161)
-Inverted Arm Bar (pg. 163)
-Kung Fu Move to Jiu-Claw (pg. 164)

RETARD CONTROL

-The Duda (pg. 146)
-The Crocodile (pg. 147)

BREAKING OPPONENT DOWN

-Non-Stop (pg. 129)
-Breaking Opponent Down
 Into Mission Control (pg. 131)
-Over/Under Hook (pg. 132)
-S-grip (pg. 133)
-To Double Under-Hooks (pg. 134)

MISSION CONTROL

-Mission Control to Pyramid (pg. 153)
-Mission Pump (to Spider Web) (pg. 141)
-Meat Hook to Triangle (pg. 143)

HAND TO MAT

-Zombie (pg. 135)
-Night of the
 Living Dead (pg. 137)
-The Exhumer (pg. 139)

NEW YORK

-The East Coast Croc (pg. 166)
-Rescue Dog (pg. 168)

FLOW CHART

TWISTER SIDE CONTROL

CLEAR THE HEAD

CHILL DOG

INVISIBLE COLLAR

JIU-CLAW

SPIDER WEB

First Published in 2006 by Victory Belt Publishing.

Copyright © 2006 Eddie Bravo, Erich Krauss & Glen Cordoza

(ISBN 13) 978-0-9777315-9-6
(ISBN 10) 0-9777315-9-6

This book is for educational purposes. The publisher and authors of this instructional book are not responsible in any manner whatsoever for any adverse effects arising directly or indirectly as a result of the information provided in this book. If not practiced safely and with caution, martial arts can be dangerous to you and to others. It is important to consult with a professional martial arts instructor before beginning training. It is also very important to consult with a physician prior to training due to the intense and strenuous nature of the techniques in this book.

Victory Belt ® is a registered trademark of Victory Belt Publishing.

10th Planet Jiu-Jitsu ® is a registered trademark of Eddie Bravo.

Printed in China

CONTENTS

Part 3: Butterfly Guard

Part 4: Rubber Guard

INVISIBLE COLLAR

JIU-CLAW

JIU-CLAW SWEEPS

TROUBLESHOOTING THE RUBBER GUARD

BREAKING GRIPS

FAILED BREAK DOWN

DEALING WITH THE STACK

DEFENDING THE SLAM

MMA TACTICS

Part 5: Spider Web

Part 6: Escapes to Guard

ESCAPES TO HALF GUARD

MOUNT TO HALF GUARD ESCAPES

SIDE CONTROL TO HALF GUARD ESCAPES

ESCAPES TO BUTTERFLY GUARD

Acknowledgments

A massive thank you goes out to Erich Krauss and Glen Cordoza for not only putting in ridiculously crazy hours helping me with this book, but also for putting this whole wonderful book deal together. You two have my greatest appreciation.

To Joe for being the Fedor of friends. No one has ever had my back like you dude.

To all my boys—Compella, Einstein, Laurence, and Tait—for being my loyal dogs, and especially for being my grappling dummies in this book.

To my master Jean Jacques for always standing behind me, even when the president of the Brazilian Jiu-Jitsu Federation was furious at me for publicly treating the gi like a three-piece suit. You will always be my master.

To the Gracie family for forever changing the face of martial arts. No family on the planet is tougher than you guys. Without your revolutionary strategies and ideas, the world of mixed martial arts would not exist and neither would this book.

To Larry Goldberg for hooking Erich and I up. Without you blowing me up to him, this book would not be.

To my mother for raising my brother, sister, and me all on a $150 a week after our evil stepfather left us. I will never forget how ecstatic you were when you got overtime on Saturdays just so you would have extra money to take us to McDonald's on payday. I love you mom!

To my biological father for very rarely being around and having zero love for me. You made me question society and humanity at an early age. Thank you. How ya like me now?

To my step dad for the physical brutality and mental beatings you gave me. Without you, my music would not

Eddie Bravo (right) with his former band Blackened Kill Symphony.

exist. When I get my first gold record, I'm gonna break it on your face.

To Jack Herer for changing my life forever with your book, *The Emperor Wears No Clothes*. If everyone on earth read your book, there would be pure harmony in all of life, all around the world. Your book can literally save the planet.

Above all, I want and need to thank the sacred plant cannabis sativa. Without this ancient medicine entering my life at twenty-eight years of age, I would not be writing this book, there would not be a Rubber Guard, and I certainly would not be creating the music I'm currently producing. If marijuana hadn't found its way into my life, I would probably be married and divorced, still deejaying at the good ol' local strip club. I know it might sound a little bit insane attributing success to an illegal substance, but it is wholeheartedly true. Marijuana has gotten a bum deal for years. It all started with government propaganda in the 1930's, and that propaganda is still alive and kicking today. I know this to be true because I had bought into it most of my life.

While growing up, several of my friends in the neighborhood religiously smoked pot. The few times I had indulged, it did little more than make me paranoid and mute. It led me to believe that smoking makes you stupid, and this assumption was reinforced by all the propaganda and the fact that several of the potheads I knew were dumb as shit. Part of my dislike for pot might even have come from my stepfather. He loved smoking, and I hated everything about him. I just couldn't see myself liking something he liked. However, there were those times throughout my teens and early twenties when I put my disdain on hold to do a little puffing. This usually occurred at some party where I felt

Go to http://www.jackherer.com for the details on the "Reefer Madness" propaganda in the 1930's sponsored by the U.S. government. It will blow you away.

extreme pressure to partake in a joint being passed around or if I thought it might get me closer to some pussy. I felt that if pot was really as good as some people claimed, then the paranoia would vanish and my voice would return. Instead I usually encountered a train wreck.

The first train wreck occurred in the eleventh grade. During lunch break at school I was pressured into taking a puff off a joint. I couldn't blame the kids who did the pressuring because everything about me screamed STONER. I had long hair, wore heavy metal shirts to school, and played drums in a trash metal band. So they did the pressuring, and I caved in. Immediately I knew I fucked up. Getting high at a party was nerve wracking enough, but now I was high at school.

I'm jacked, I thought. *How the hell am I going to make it through the rest of the day?*

I had U.S. History after lunch, and I walked into class high as the sky and paranoid as fuck that the teacher would figure out that I was stoned. *Don't say a word*, I thought. *Don't move a muscle. Just sit in your chair and look forward, no one will ever figure you out.*

Boy was I wrong. A couple of kids that sat in front of me kept looking back and tripping out on me. I wasn't saying or doing anything out of the ordinary, so I couldn't figure out why they kept staring. Then one of the kids spoke.

"Dude, your eyes are devil red," he said.

Another kid turned around. "Yeah, your eyes are on fire."

I didn't think they were telling the truth, but then some girl gave me her compact mirror thingy and I took a look at my eyes. I totally freaked out. You see, my eyes are hazel, but they get bright green when I cry or they get irritated. When I looked into the mirror, the whites of my eyes were as red as Santa's coat and the insides were as green as a Christmas tree.

Without thinking or saying a word, I got up, walked out of the class, and headed straight to the restroom. I didn't know what the hell I was going to do—I just knew I had to get out of that classroom with those eyes. I sat down on the bathroom floor and went crazy in my head. I guess my teacher didn't like me excusing myself from class because a few minutes later the campus cop walked into the shitter. Not sure how to handle the situation, I quickly started crying and pretending that I was sick. It was all I could think of on such short notice.

The cop picked me up by the shoulder and walked me to the principal's office. The cop had been around a block or two, wasn't buying into my sick story in the slightest, but luckily the principal did and he let me go home. When I finally arrived at my house, I crawled into bed and stared at the clock on my VCR. I watched the minutes creep by, waiting for the dreaded high to be over with. I hated weed.

I had not forgotten my traumatic experience when I took another puff off a joint at the age of twenty-six. My reason for caving this time was the hope of getting laid. This stripper I had been trying to bang for quite some time finally made it over to my house for some wine and a Blockbuster evening. She pulled out a joint. Not wanting her to think I was a square, I took a couple of rips. On the outside I pretended that it wasn't a big deal, but on the inside I knew I had just fucked myself yet again.

There we were, both lying in my bed at the beginning of the movie. I was so high I didn't talk, didn't make a move. My mind was on fire, yet I couldn't do anything. After laying frozen next to her for about an hour, she got up, grabbed her stuff, and bolted out the door without a word. I was too paralyzed to try and stop her, so I just lay there in a coma, wondering what the hell had just happened and blaming weed for ruining a vagina moment. I hated weed more than ever.

It wasn't until June of 1998 that my whole perception changed. At the time my best friend James, who happened to also be my music partner and the rapper in my band Blackened Kill Symphony, had been diagnosed with cancer. His brutal bout with chemotherapy caused a severe brain hemorrhage that put him in a coma for days. I actually thought he was dead for a while there, but like a savage warrior he pulled himself out of the jaws of death and survived. I had been writing music with James since I was sixteen, and I had never imagined being involved in a music project without him. We were like blood brothers with the greatest songwriting chemistry possible. But the physical damage caused by the chemo left him unable to continue his musical dreams with me. Mentally he was still the same ol' James—you would never know anything was wrong with him—but physically. . . Let's put it this way, he would never be able to drive a car again and he would forever be on some serious anti-seizure meds.

What was I to do? Continue with the Blackened Kill Symphony formula, rap, metal and Goth? Try something new? Fuck, I didn't know what the hell I was gonna do. It just didn't seem right doing anything without James.

Life had fallen into a sinkhole. Thank the baby Jesus for jiu-jitsu. That wonderful game of strangulation and joint destruction took my mind off my musical crisis. So did romance at my job. I'd been working at a strip club for five years and had dated quite a few of the dancers. Some hot, some not so hot, and one or two so bad that I didn't dare tell the guys at the club about for fear of total humiliation. I went from one girlfriend to another, just like I had been doing since the age of thirteen. Some girls lasted longer than others, but ninety nine percent of my relationships went the same way: Lust then infatuation, love then suffocation. I always ended up feeling trapped, confined, and burned out after a few months of bliss, but I couldn't put my finger on why I kept going through this same alcohol-like routine of getting drunk with love then feeling miserable later. I just kept repeating the cycle blindly. Despite the distraction these relationships offered, the bitter cycle only got more intense the longer I went without making music.

Then Darian started working at the club. Her body was so amazing that guys were talking about her ass in clubs miles away. Her tits were teeny-tiny, but she had played soccer in Kentucky for most of her life, which had crafted a spectacular behind and pair of legs. Women who spent their adolescence playing soccer, cheerleading, riding horses, running track, or doing ballet usually drive me crazy, and Darian was no exception. I felt like I needed a psychiatrist the first time I laid my eyes on her big juicy ass. And she had a beautiful face to go along with the body, so I was in some serious love. We hit it off right away.

About two or three weeks into the relationship, when our infatuation was at its peak, I was at a nightclub with my buddy Scott Redondo. Darian was working at the strip club that night, and I couldn't get my mind off her. This was especially true after Scott and me took some ecstasy. When I couldn't stand being without her any longer, I called her up. I asked her to leave work and come meet me at the club. I said I was blowing the fuck up on E and all I could think about was kissing and squeezing and dancing and fucking the shit out of her.

When Darian got to the club, she immediately asked if I could get some more E, but the place was bone dry. We ended up going back to my place, where I made a round of phone calls, but there was no ecstasy to be found. Finally we gave up and Darian pulled out a joint one of her strip club customers had given her. She wasn't that into pot, but at that point, she thought a weed high was better than no high at all. But she refused to smoke by herself.

"Hell no, I'm not smoking that shit!" I spouted when I saw her looking over at me.

"Please," she whispered, "I'm not going to smoke unless you do."

I tried and tried to convince her to puff without me, but she wasn't budging. It was late, my E-high had worn off, and I was feeling so great sitting there with her that eventually I caved in. "Fuck it," I said. "Let's do it."

We laughed all through the night and straight into dawn, most of the time for no good reason. It was like we were on laughing gas that some insane scientist from another planet had concocted. We called up Scott but didn't have anything to say to him; we just took turns laughing at the top of our lungs into the phone. It was magically amazing.

The next day I couldn't stop thinking about and analyzing the night before. Why didn't the weed make me paranoid and introverted? Why didn't it have the same negative effect on me that it always had before? At the age of twenty-eight, I'd had a wonderful experience smoking pot for the first time. Was it the E that was still in my system from hours earlier? *Maybe*, I thought to myself. But there was only one way to find out for sure—smoke some more!

So we smoked again the next night, and again we had a beautiful experience. We finished the rest of that joint, stayed home, laughed like children, ordered pizza with cheesecake, and ate like wild savages. We were in heaven. Two potheads were born.

The next day, after breaking down my life for the past twenty-four hours, I finally realized why we had such a great time smoking pot. We were in total love. We were already on top of the world. Marijuana doesn't make you feel good or bad, it just amplifies your emotions. It makes you feel more of what you're already feeling. That was the conclusion of my self-analysis. I thought to myself, 'That must be the reason you felt so paranoid smoking ganja growing up.' My whole life I always thought of myself as a strong-minded kid who wasn't fazed by the lack of love in my family. But the more I broke down my life that day, the more I began to see that I was really just a super insecure little boy. I had always felt sorry for myself because my biological father was never around and because my stepfather physically and mentally tortured me. Yeah, that was Eddie, a pathetic, lost soul who disguised all his fragile emotions by creating dark and evil music. All of a sudden it was clear how fucked up I was growing up. I figured that must have been the reason I had bad trips every time I tried pot.

From that day on, my life would never be the same. Along with a complete and constant analysis of my life, weed made my brain go crazy with ideas, strategies, and artistic flow. All of a sudden I understood stand-up comedy. I had always been a huge fan of stand-up comedy, but I never had any idea how comedians came up with their material. To me it was like magic. I didn't have a clue how to deliver jokes on stage or create an SNL-type sketch. I loved the hell out of it, but I never knew how they came up with that shit. During high school I had been a master at cracking up my classmates. As a matter of fact, I was so good at cracking them up that I gave two of my teachers, Ms. Franklin and Ms. Aspen, nervous breakdowns that caused them to retire. But cracking jokes in high school was different than getting on stage with seasoned bits and delivering time and again. A good comedian can make you laugh way harder than any movie, and how they did that had always been a mystery to me.

But when I was high, it started to make sense. Without even trying, comedy sketches and stand-up material started flowing through my head. For a good six months after I started smoking pot, I was too afraid to drive stoned, so when I smoked, it was always at night in my home. I just sat there, tripping the hell out on my brain activity. Every time I came up with a comedy idea, I would write it down on one of my two dry-marker message boards. Within a couple of months, both boards were filled with chicken scratches. Most of the comedy ideas I came up with were far from funny—in fact, quite a few of my ideas were terrible. But I did end up writing and ghetto-producing one sketch about a white guy named Quatoof who wanted to be a thugged-out black guy so bad he wore heavy, dark makeup and afroed out his hair. He got away with wearing the makeup by telling everyone that he had the same skin disease as Michael Jackson—except his facial spots were black instead of white. And if you questioned him about the makeup, you would probably end up a missing person. Like all non-black people who wish they were gangsta rappers, Quatoof was in mad denial and a violent criminal. His mother had moved them to Compton when he was ten so she could shack up with her pimp boyfriend, who took it

upon himself to whore her out for crack, and it didn't take long for Quatoof to become the most violent criminal on the mean streets.

I know you're probably thinking, *What the fuck*!! It would make a lot more sense if you saw the sketch. If you're interested, you can find it as a bonus feature on my Twister DVD. You might even be able to find it on Google. Anyway, the reason I brought it up at all is because smoking allowed me to come up with that crazy sketch, and that crazy sketch later helped me land a job as a writer on Comedy Central's *The Man Show*. Smoking also gave me the creativity to come up with an entire act, which I threw down on stage at some open-mic nights at The Comedy Store in Los Angeles.

Understanding the mechanics of comedy was only one example of how marijuana was beginning to rebuild my mind. It was like my brain had gotten a supercharger installed. And with that supercharger having allowed me to reach a fairly high level in the world of comedy in a short period of time, I began to wonder what would happen if I harnessed all its creative power into my music. After all, music was the most important thing in my life. Realizing that continuing to run with the comedy ball would inevitably take away from my music, I quit my job at The Man Show and stopped going up on stage after just nine shows. I was ready to embed myself in a world of music.

The Music

I've been creating music since the age of thirteen, and up until 1998 I never imagined trying to perform while stoned. I never understood how musicians, including some of my band mates, could climb on stage and play when faded. All I had to think about was how paranoid, insecure, and insane I felt the couple of times I had gotten pressured into smoking to realize I couldn't do that. I thought there would be no way I could play an instrument under the influence of ganja, not a fucking chance.

So instead of producing music with the magic of cannabis, I co-wrote all my material with the deep-rooted insecurities created by my loveless childhood. I was basically trying to create the soundtrack for this dark, evil, dominating character that I wanted everyone to believe that I was. The first real band I was in was a satanic speed metal group called Execrate. It meant to put someone under a spell, or maybe it was to declare someone evil. It was something like that. Anyhow, the point is that I was down with the darkness. It wasn't like I was that far out of bounds. When it came to heavy metal and speed metal in the early eighties, Satan was a very popular song topic. No one actually worshipped Satan. I didn't even believe that this evil god existed. It was just in vogue to scare people musically, kind of like writing horror movies.

By the time I was sixteen, I had written a host of super fast, satanic, nuclear doom songs with vocal melodies that sounded like Zombie Raptor, and I decided that I had outgrown Execrate. I formed a new band called Resistance. In my mind Satan was played out, so I decided to shift gears. I could have chosen to write from the heart, but instead I still wrote from the skin. It was as if I was trying to express myself solely through what I wore rather than through my soul. What people saw in my music was more important than what they felt. I wanted people to see a visual picture when they heard my music. I didn't even know you could write music that would actually make people *feel* the pictures inside of you. When band members said that they wrote off 'feel', I thought they were too lazy to take the time to perfect the picture they were trying to project with their music. To me, writing off feel seemed like writing off the top of your head, and how good could that be? So I stuck to my game plan and constructed songs that were insanely long and had many, many parts. Trying to impress people with my songwriting ability, I put together tunes that were eight minutes, nine minutes, and ten minutes long, each with about seventeen riffs and mad tempo changes.

The music I produced in Resistance was still dark and heavy, just not as noisy as Execrate and a lot more polished. I finally had a real vocalist in my band that could actually sing in key. Even though I wrote most of the lyrics, he taught me a lot about vocal melodies. Instead of devil songs, I wrote songs about anti-organized religion, world economic disasters, and violent uprisings. I even started adding keyboards to Resistance, which was taboo in speed metal back in the 80's. I knew a drummer, Butch, who could play drums with one hand and keyboards with the other, and it totally blew me away. So I tried to do the same in Resistance, but I sucked at it. Playing drums and keyboards at the same time is like trying to make three girls cum at the exact same moment. Possible, but only a microscopic percentage of the population has the patience and ability to actually pull it off. But why was I trying to add keyboards to my speed metal band?

On the outside I was a total metal head. I had hair down to my waist and a different evil concert shirt for everyday of the week. So I felt I had to create music that represented my image. But on the inside, hidden deep within my soul, was this new wave/Goth lover. I was secretly into The Cure, Depeche Mode, Sisters of Mercy, and even some wimpy shit like Billy Idol and Duran Duran. As a teen back in the 80's, you could only openly claim one style—metal, new wave, ska, punk, etc. That's just the way it was back then, and in some circles that kind of stupidity still exists today. I knew some new wave/ska dudes in junior high who were secretly into Iron Maiden and Def Leopard. I was starting to sneak my hidden influences into my music with the whole keyboard/drum thing I was trying to do in Resistance. But still, my music mostly catered to my fragile ego and remained fast, heavy, and cloaked in darkness.

By the end of the 80's, I was fully burned out on the brutality and anger of speed metal and wanted to make big changes. I never had been a huge fan of hip hop, but when I heard Anthrax and Public Enemy come together to do 'Bring the Noise,' my head nearly exploded. Sure Run DMC had mixed guitar with rap years earlier, but that was AC/DCish rock. This was extra heavy and crunchy. In fact, Anthrax was one of the pioneers of speed metal. I wasn't into rap mainly because most of the music was sampled from old funk songs or jazz songs or disco hits from the 70's. All of which are genres of music that usually don't harmonize with the notes in my DNA. I just don't feel it. But hearing Chuck D's rap over Anthrax's heavy music made my blood bubble over with inspiration. I thought, 'How fucking insane would it be if there was a whole album with songs like Bring the Noise?' I thought it would be even more insane if Goth-style keyboards, synthetic drums, crazy samples, and sound effects were also mixed in. It would be off the hook!

Immediately I started experimenting with rap on the side, but after a couple of months, I decided to make those big changes in my life. Finally fed up with super fast drum beats, I quit Resistance, sold my ten piece Tama Swingstar drum set, bought a new electric guitar, moved to Hollywood, decided to be a guitar player/singer, and formed the band that I mentioned at the beginning of my weed story, Blackened Kill Symphony. I started the band of my dreams, which happened to be the only band of its kind back in 1991. It had heavy guitars, big acoustic drums, big synthetic drums, live bass, synthetic bass, lots of Gothish synth, piano, samples, strings draped with abrasive indus- trial vocals, and a separate rapper. It was kind of like what Linkin Park is doing today, except they were probably in the 4th grade back then. At the time, Faith No More was the only band close to our sound, but they didn't have a rapper. The singer of Faith No More rapped on occasion, but no one in the rap industry ever acknowledged him as a rapper. That's like calling Anthony Keidis from the Red Hot Chili Peppers a rapper. Rage Against The Machine had legit rap over rock, but they didn't use any synthesizer or synthetic drums. We were certainly one of a kind.

I thought we were going to be huge. There was no way this formula could fail. Combining the elements of metal, Goth, and rap would be the next big thing, I was sure of it. Ten years later the formula would prove to be a winner thanks to Linkin Park.

The reason Blackened Kill Symphony (BKS) didn't skyrocket was because my ego and insecurities held the group back. Even though I had evolved dramatically from my speed metal days (dropping the fast drums and white noise was huge), I was still obsessed with creating very long songs with way too many parts. I even went so far as to write an eleven-minute song. Why? Maybe it had a little to do with my manic self- consciousness. Techni- cally, I wasn't a virtuoso at any instrument. I never gave a shit about practicing scales, playing lead guitar, or putting together a five-minute drum solo. I didn't shred on guitar or drums or keyboards; I just put it all together. All that mattered to me was arranging and producing songs, so I felt I had to show the world that even though there were tens of thousands of guitars players that could play more notes per minute than I could, most of them couldn't create these crazy epic songs that I was putting together. How sad of me. Ten years later Linkin Park had it right. The right for- mula, AND the right song arrangements. No long, drawn- out songs with a million different changes, just two or three parts that fucking rock for about three to four minutes. No bullshit, no showing off, just killer vibes and hypnotic grooves. Vibe and groove were definitely two things that were foreign to my music back then. . . That is until 1998, the year weed rescued my music.

When I became a pothead at twenty-eight, BKS had just broken up and James, my best friend and the rapper in the band, had cancer. I didn't have a clue what direction to take with my music, but within days of my first enjoyable puff, my music seriously started to change. All of a sudden,

I realized how much my ego had hurt BKS. It took getting high to figure out why my band had broken apart. I was trying too hard to impress everyone with complex songs, and I wasn't writing from within. I hid behind my music like it was a mask—a dominating mask of darkness and false strength. Marijuana made me come to the conclusion that even though I thought I was too strong to be affected by my loveless childhood, I was in fact heavily battered by it. It was all right there in my music, plain for me to see. A lonely, scared little boy disguised in gladiator attire.

Immediately I dropped the electric guitar and got ob- sessed with the acoustic guitar. I hardly ever picked up the electric back then, and my synthesizer was starting to fill more and more holes in my music. For the first time in my life, I began to understand what playing with 'feel' meant. No more violence and destruction, just my soul pouring out from within. That beaten child that had been locked inside of me was finally being released in the form of my melo- dies. Weed was like magic to me. I would smoke a bowl and songs would just flow out from my heart. I even started writing music with a female singer, Gina. My ex-band mates probably freaked the fuck out when they first heard of that. Some of them may have even thought of me as a 'sellout', but to me it was all about finally being able to give life to the melodies that had been suffocating inside me.

We called ourselves Face Down, and Gina and I would smoke weed before every writing and recording session. We would write song after song. They were ballady, melan- choly songs, but with a sense of overcoming. Like I said, all of my locked-up childhood cries were oozing out of my pores. There was so much detoxing to be done.

It was the most significant change in my life, and the wonderful effects of cannabis brought it all on. If you listen to any BKS song, and then you listen to any Face Down song, you will see irrefutable evidence of the artis- tic power that marijuana provides. Nowadays, I wouldn't even consider writing, producing, performing, recording, or mixing without first taking a few inhalations of the magic plant known to some as reefer. I use it as a tool for produc- ing music, just like an athlete uses human growth hormone to compete on a professional level. He can definitely play without it, but he would never be able to reach his full po- tential. Weed is like a steroid for the imagination, except no one has ever died of marijuana, ever.

After about 3 years of writing ballads with Gina, we split up. Even though I loved the music I wrote with Face

Down more than any other band I was in, Gina and I had some serious personal differences, so I broke the project up. Since then, over the last couple of years, I've pulled out my electric guitar and been feeling the BKS vibe again. I even found this amazing rapper, Compella, who also happens to be a mad stoner. But now I'm doing the whole heavy hip-hop thing right. Right from the soul. I've been remixing all the Face Down songs into rap, and it sounds awesome to me. I love it even more than the original Face Down versions. The heaviness is back, but this time the crunch of my guitar is molded together with cannabis. It's the same old skool BKS formula—rap, metal, and Goth—but without the ego. Just the pure honest emotions that came out while I was with Face Down, with some mad power injected into the backbone of the music. I even brought my vocals back. The project is called 'compella and the twister,' and if you myspace me at www.myspace.com/thetwister, I'll send you a demo. We even have a song called "put ur weed up".

Relationships

I also have marijuana to thank for some dramatic improvements in my love life. Like many people in today's society, I went from one girlfriend to the next. Since the age of thirteen, there had been a clear and distinct pattern with most of my girlfriends, and this pattern became painfully obvious when stoned. I would fall in love with a girl, and she would fall in love with me. We'd go galloping through heaven for a while, but then the badness would begin. First we would begin to smother each other with jealousy and insecurity, then I would want out, then she would fall apart, then I would be stuck in a horrible mess of tears and misery. Then I would start all over again with some new girl, and on and on.

Once I started smoking weed, I realized that I didn't want or need to go through that shit anymore. Keeping my girlfriends happy took so much of my time and effort, and I was at a point in my life where I really needed to put the pedal to the metal with my music. Between working, jiu-jitsu, and a full-time girlfriend, I had little time left over for my music. And that's where I wanted to spend all of my time. I was twenty-eight and felt I had to make some serious changes in the way I handled my social life. It was all about total freedom—freedom to work on my music whenever I wanted with no grief. Freedom to do whatever I wanted, whenever I wanted, with no questions asked.

Total freedom became my total focus. If I wanted to make it in the music business, I had to make some life altering decisions. It certainly wasn't easy. After Darian and I finally got through the 'tears and misery' part of our relationship, I got sucked into one more. She was even more beautiful than Darian, including her legs and ass. As a matter of fact, to this day, no other girl has rocked my world sexually like this one. Her pussy and body and sexuality had me under a spell. I called her Voodoo. To top it off, her personality was far superior to Darian's as well. She got me good; I was hooked like a junkie.

After Voodoo had the chains locked around me, I began to see the mess I had walked into yet again. I thought I was getting myself off the hook by telling her that I didn't want a serious relationship. At least once a week I told her that I wasn't her boyfriend. She would even say the same shit back to me, telling me how she didn't want to be committed or be my girlfriend. So I thought everything should have been as right as rain. I would have a steady lay, and I would also have my freedom.

What I didn't realize at the time is that after seeing a girl three or four days in a row a couple of times, she automatically becomes your girlfriend. It doesn't matter how many times you tell her that you ain't her boyfriend. When you invest that kind of time into each other, you can't help but get attached and fall in love. So I had another girlfriend. Like all the others, it was quite wonderful in the beginning, but once I began to see through the fog, see how my new life of total freedom had already gone to shit, the 'tears and misery' part soon followed. I learned my lesson on that one, and I haven't had a girlfriend since. That was August of 2000. Six fucking years! Whoa! Sometimes I can't believe it. I will admit that I do sometimes miss the little things that come with having a girlfriend, like cuddling, watching television together, and hitting a Sunday afternoon movie and dinner, but my true, total freedom outweighs that by a thousand pounds. The magic of cannabis made me understand that the only way I was going to take my music and jiu-jitsu to the next level was with absolute freedom.

I decided that I could no longer give into my insecurities and let the primal instinct of jealousy and possessiveness control me. Nor would I ever allow any girl or person to control me. Why is everyone on the planet all about having a volunteer parole officer living with them? In a ganja filled state, I came to the conclusion that jealousy and possessiveness were nothing more than ancient DNA programs—programs designed by mother nature when the survival of the human race was uncertain. Passing your DNA on was the only goal back then. Violence from jealousy was necessary to wipe out competition in the wild that could threaten the passing of your DNA. But nowadays there is no longer the need for jealousy and possessiveness. The world is way too overpopulated with humans. We rule the planet. That instinct needs to be extinct.

When most people get jealous, they have no idea why there body is reacting that way. They just react and let those negative emotions rule their actions and mental state. I have decided to let that all go. I have decided to never let my relationships with women affect me in a negative way. I am treating everyone like friends from now until the day I die, or until I meet some girl that puts a wicked Jedi mind spell on me. Who knows, anything can happen I guess, but I doubt it. My social life since 2000 has been a series of non-committed relationships that produce a mess of positivity and very little negativity. I've never been happier with my life.

Ganja and Jiu-Jitsu

The last major change in my life that was brought on by cannabis had to do with jiu-jitsu. During the first six months of my pothead era, there were a lot of things that I never considered doing high. These things including driving, reading a book, paying bills, and most definitely climbing onto the mats and training jiu-jitsu. When stoned, I was pretty much scared to death of doing anything but chilling at my house, ordering food, and writing down ideas. Going to the academy and rolling seemed suicidal to me.

I was under the assumption that weed would slow my game down, and sense I was small and feeble back then (I didn't get into lifting weights until years later), I thought caffeine drinks were the way to go. I believed that I needed an energy rush to survive on the mats. But when I was sitting at home high as fuck, I couldn't stop breaking down my jiu-jitsu game, as well as breaking down the games of those competing in MMA and no-gi jiu-jitsu tournaments. It didn't take long to realize that my constant analysis of submission set-ups without the gi, as well as my revelations about how the gi affected no-gi grappling, was always ignited by the ancient green brain food. Still, the idea of rolling stoned never seemed beneficial.

Then one of the top jiu-jitsu players on the planet told me that he rolled stoned all the time. He tried to convince me that when he trained baked, he flowed smoother because his techniques were driven by instinct. He told me that he was flat out better when he was high. It shocked the hell out of me, and I quickly reevaluated my thoughts about rolling under the guidance of weed. However, the next day I didn't smoke a fat bowl before heading to practice. I might have if I didn't train in the morning. At the time I only smoked at night, so it was quite easy for me to avoid mixing the two.

But when I opened my own school years later, that all changed. I taught class at 8:30pm, and at this point in my life I was in the habit of smoking at around five or six in the afternoon. I considered putting smoking off until after class was over, but then I remembered what that top jiu-jitsu player had told me. So I tried it out, and he was absolutely right. I never rolled better in my life. It took a little while to forget the fact that I was actually training stoned, but when that cleared up, my jiu-jitsu was off the hook. It was so amazing that very rarely do I train without cannabis in my system to this day. Not only do I train stoned, but I also teach all of my classes stoned.

I could go on and on about how having THC consistently in my brain has affected my jiu-jitsu game, but if it's not painfully obvious to you that the 10th Planet Jiu-Jitsu style was developed by a hardcore stoner, then you're definitely not paying attention.

The Emperor Wears No Clothes

To think I almost quit smoking pot after the first six months. I almost quit because I thought I had to be doing some kind of brain and lung damage. Isn't that what we're taught to believe?

I remember this phone conversation I had with a good friend of mine named Marie. She watched me turn into a stoner right in front of her eyes and was sort of feeling sorry for me. I told her, "I know, I know Marie. I know I should quit, but when I smoke pot, my mind is flooded with ideas, concepts, and strategies. It's changing the way I think about everything in my life, including the most important thing in my life, my music."

"You're just using pot as a crutch," she told me. "You should really quit now before it ruins your life"

I seriously thought about it. After all, did I really want to risk getting lung cancer? Thankfully I didn't up and quit. I decided to give pot and the creativity it generated a little more time. I just kept smoking and breaking down my little universe, thinking that it was causing me all sorts of harm. Then I met Kaya, a stripper who started working at the club to pay her boyfriend's legal fees. He was well known in the hemp activist movement and had been imprisoned for doing research on the medicinal uses of cannabis. Kaya would always say the craziest shit about weed—positive, too-good-to-be-true shit about weed. The activism her boyfriend was involved in had worn off on her in a big way, and she would always offer me this insane info about the medicinal and industrial uses of weed. Even though I was a pothead, I didn't know the history behind it, like how, when, and why it became illegal. All I knew is that pot came from a street dealer and it was bad for your health.

I thought hemp activists were hyping the industrial uses of hemp to justify the inhalation of its female flowers. She would tell me about these long road trips that she would take totally stoned, and how she loved to read books high and do research on the computer. At that point, early in my pothead days, I couldn't understand how she could drive for eight hours while high, much less study books. The first time I drove stoned, I drove two miles and was terrified as fuck. It was 10:45pm and the video stored closed at eleven. I had five overdue tapes that needed to be returned in fifteen minutes or I would have to pay serious penalties. The video store was only a few minutes away, but I was stoned as fuck and thought there was no way I could make it. I went back and forth for a few minutes, and then I said fuck it. I didn't want to pay those hefty late fees. So I took a few deep breaths and took a chance.

It was one scary trip. There was an intersection that had no signal, and it took me forever to cross. I was horrified that I would lose control and crash. Eventually I made it home, and then I sat on my couch for about an hour, totally amazed that I made it back alive. How the hell was Kaya able to drive, read, and study stoned?

She kept telling me about this book that I needed to read, 'The Emperor Wears No Clothes.' She said that everything she was trying to tell me would make sense once I read this book. *Hhhhmmmm*, I thought. *Perhaps I will get*

around to reading it one day, but she sounds a little crazy and you still need to quit.

That Christmas, Marie asked me what I wanted, and I thought about it for a minute. I remembered the book Kaya kept telling me about, so that is what I told Marie that I wanted. When Christmas rolled around, she threw me the book and said, "Here you go stoner, Merry Christmas. But I still think you should quit."

The moment I got home, I sat down and opened the book. Immediately I was obsessed. I couldn't put it down. I did, however, slam the book down on the floor every five minutes or so. Not in disgust for the book or weed, but in disgust at how our government has brainwashed us all to think marijuana is bad for you.

'We have all been bamboozled!' I thought to myself.

I discovered that in the 1930's, Harry Anslinger, America's first drug czar, convinced the people of this country that marijuana made you kill people, as well as made white women want to have orgies with blacks and Mexicans. He was all about putting fear into the minds of all Americans so that he could have marijuana outlawed. He spread the fear through government-funded movies and fake newspaper reports. Sounds insane, right? But it's 100% true. Go to www.jackherer.com and order the book, it will blow you the fuck away. I found out that the real reason Harry Anslinger was trying to outlaw pot was not because he wanted to protect people, but rather for economic reasons. He wanted to make hemp illegal because of its amazing industrial uses. You see, hemp has been humanity's number one plant for thousands of years.

From: The Emperor Wears No Clothes

From more than 1,000 years before the time of Christ until 1883 A.D., cannabis hemp - indeed, marijuana - was our planet's largest agricultural crop and most important industry, involving thousands of products and enterprises; producing the overall majority of Earth's fiber, fabric, lighting oil, paper, incense and medicines. In addition, it was a primary source of essential food oil and protein for humans and animals.

In 1619, America's first marijuana law was enacted at Jamestown Colony, Virginia, "ordering" all farmers to "make tryal of" (grow) Indian hempseed. More mandatory (must-grow) hemp cultivation laws were enacted in Massachusetts in 1631, in Connecticut in 1632 and in the Chesapeake Colonies into the mid-1700s.

Even in England, the much-sought-after prize of full British citizenship was bestowed by a decree of the crown on foreigners who would grow cannabis, and fines were often levied against those who refused.

Cannabis hemp was legal tender (money) in most of the Americas from 1631 until the early 1800s. Why? To encourage American farmers to grow more.

You could pay your taxes with cannabis hemp throughout America for over 200 years.

You could even be jailed in America for not growing cannabis during several periods of shortage, e.g., in Virginia between 1763 and 1767. (Herndon, G.M., Hemp in Colonial Virginia, 1963; The Chesapeake Colonies, 1954; L.A. Times, August 12, 1981; et al.)

George Washington and Thomas Jefferson grew cannabis on their plantations. Jefferson,3 while envoy to France, went to great expense - and even considerable risk to himself and his secret agents - to procure particularly good hempseeds smuggled illegally into Turkey from China. The Chinese Mandarins (political rulers) so valued their hempseed that they made its exportation a capital offense.

The United States Census of 1850 counted 8,327 hemp "plantations"* (minimum 2,000-acre farm) growing cannabis hemp for cloth, canvas and even the cordage used for baling cotton. Most of these plantations were located in the South or in the border states, primarily because of the cheap slave labor available prior to 1865 for the labor-intensive hemp industry.

Benjamin Franklin started one of America's first paper mills with cannabis. This allowed America to have a free colonial press without having to beg or justify the need for paper and books from England.

In addition, various marijuana and hashish extracts were the first, second and third most prescribed medicines in the United States from 1842 until the 1890s. It's medicinal use continued legally through the 1930s for humans and figured even more prominently in American and world veterinary medicines during this time.

Cannabis extract medicines were produced by Eli Lilly, Parke-Davis, Tildens, Brothers Smith (Smith Brothers), Squibb and many other American and European companies and apothecaries. During all that time there was not one reported death from cannabis extract medicines, and virtually no abuse or mental disorders reported, except for first-time or novice users occasionally becoming disoriented or overly introverted.

Why has cannabis hemp/marijuana been so important in history? Because cannabis hemp is, overall, the strongest, most-durable, longest-lasting natural soft-fiber on the planet. Its leaves and flower tops (marijuana) were - depending on the culture - the first, second or third most important and most used medicines for two-thirds of the world's people for at least 3,000 years, until the turn of the century.

Botanically, hemp is a member of the most advanced plant family on Earth. It is a dioecious (having male, female and sometimes hermaphroditic - male and female on the same plant), woody, herbaceous annual that uses the sun more efficiently than virtually any other plant on our planet, reaching a robust 12 to 20 feet or more in one short growing sea-

1. Jack Herer, "The Emperor Wears No Clothes."
   Available at: http://www.Jackherer.com

son. It can be grown in virtually any climate or soil condition on Earth, even marginal ones.

Hemp is, by far, Earth's premier, renewable natural resource. This is why hemp is so very important.1

So in a nutshell, when slavery was abolished in the mid 1800's, the hemp industry went into a deep decline. All of a sudden, hemp went from being the number one plant on earth to slowly falling into a downward spiral of obscurity by the late 1800's. There were no machines yet invented that could harvest hemp; cheap human labor was the only way. Fabric was way easier to manufacture with cotton because a machine that could cheaply harvest cotton had already been invented; the cotton gin. Paper started being processed using wood pulp instead of hemp. And at the turn of the century, the industrial revolution was ruled by the mastery of fossil fuel. Hemp was a lost memory in the U.S. by the 1920's, but like all plants on the planet should be, it was still very legal. Just no one in America really thought about it. It was just a plant.

That is until 1937. That's right. The U.S. government actually decided to outlaw a plant. But why would hemp be made illegal? It doesn't make any sense, right? How can a plant be illegal? Well, read *The Emperor Wears No Clothes* and find out how the big American companies and key government figures conspired to make hemp illegal after a German scientist invented the first harvesting machine made specifically for hemp. The re-emergence of hemp would be a serious threat to big business.

In the 1930's, there were a whole shit load of U.S. government sponsored films produced to make the public believe that smoking 'the evil Mexican weed' marijuana made you kill, made you insane, and made white women want to fuck blacks and Mexicans. This is all real shit! 'Reefer Madness' is the name of the most popular propaganda movie made in the thirties. That is one of the funniest movies ever. Fuck Team America, this movie had dudes smoking pot and acting like they were on PCP, except they weren't trying to make you laugh.

The people with the real power in this country wanted to scare people about the effects of marijuana so everyone would agree to outlaw it. Everyone thought they were outlawing a dangerous substance. Most people had no idea they were actually being tricked into outlawing a plant that was about to crush the already giant industries that be. Like the oil industry, the cotton industry, and the paper industry.

You gotta read the details of all this shit, it's shocking, it's enlightening, and it's mutha fuckin infuriating! I tripped balls when I found out that no one has ever died from marijuana. It freaked me out. I thought for sure people had died from pot. I mean, it's illegal, right? If it has never killed anyone, then why would it be illegal? I found out that cigarettes kill 400,000 people a FUCKING YEAR! Alcohol kills 150,000 a year, and it is also responsible for 50% of all highway deaths and 65% of all murders! And pot, zero.

It stunned me when I discovered that pot has never caused one case of lung cancer, and it sent me for a loop when I discovered that it was an amazing, all purpose medicine with a gazillion therapeutic uses, including helping those with glaucoma and asthma. And what really tripped me out was when I found out that it's actually a LUNG CLEANER AND EXPECTORANT! Fuck! How brainwashed are we?

From: The Emperor Wears No Clothes

Cannabis is the best natural expectorant to clear the human lungs of smog, dust and the phlegm associated with tobacco use. Marijuana smoke effectively dilates the airways of the lungs, the bronchi, opening them to allow more oxygen into the lungs. It is also the best natural dilator of the tiny airways of the lungs, the bronchial tubes - making cannabis the best overall bronchial dilator for 80% of the population (the remaining 20% sometimes show minor negative reactions). (See section on asthma - a disease that closes these passages in spasms - UCLA Tashkin studies, 1969-97; U.S. Costa Rican, 1980-82; Jamaican studies 1969-74, 76.) Statistical evidence - showing up consistently as anomalies in matched populations - indicates that people who smoke tobacco cigarettes are usually better off and will live longer if they smoke cannabis moderately, too. (Jamaicna, Costa Rican studies.) Millions of Americans have given up or avoided smoking tobacco products in favor of cannabis, which is not good news to the powerful tobacco lobby - Senator Jesse Helms and his cohorts. A turn-of-the-century grandfather clause in U.S. tobacco law allows 400 to 6,000 additional chemicals to be added. Additions since then to the average tobacco cigarette are unknown, and the public in the U.S. has no right to know what they are. Many joggers and marathon runners feel cannabis use cleans their lungs, allowing better endurance. The evidence indicates that cannabis use will probably increase these outlaw American marijuana-users' lives by about one to two years - yet they may lose their rights, property, children, state licenses, etc., just for using that safest of substances: cannabis. 2

Craaaaazy ass shit, right? Then I found out that artists from all genres use cannabis as a tool for creativity. Even though that part of the book wasn't much of a shocker, it was very important to me because it validated what I had been telling Marie and all my friends about the creative powers of marijuana.

From: The Emperor Wears No Clothes

Many artists and writers have used cannabis for creative stimulation - from the writers of the world's religious masterpieces to our most irreverent satirists. These include Lewis Carroll and his hookah- smoking caterpillar in Alice in Wonderland, plus Victor Hugo and Alexander Dumas; such jazz greats as Louis Armstrong, Cab Calloway, Duke Ellington and Gene Krupa; and the pattern continues right up to modern-day artists and musicians such as the Beatles, the Rolling Stones, the Eagles, the Doobie Brothers, Bob Marley, Jefferson Airplane, Willie Nelson, Buddy Rich, Country Joe & the Fish, Joe Walsh, David Carradine, David Bowie, Iggy Pop, Lola Falana, Hunter S. Thompson, Peter Tosh, the Grateful Dead, Cypress Hill, Sinead O' Connor, Black Crowes, ect. 3

I immediately went out and bought a documentary called 'The Emperor Of Hemp,' which is about Jack Herer's life. I found it fascinating that Jack Herer was totally against marijuana for most of his young adult life just like me. He was a hardcore republican, served in the military as a military police officer, and thought hippies were all lazy losers. It wasn't until the age of thirty-five that he saw the light and began to wave the marijuana flag. So much in the documentary made perfect sense, and once again our slimy government and the lies it perpetrates blew me away. I told Marie that the book and documentary had changed the way I viewed the world and life itself, but she just laughed and thought I was losing my mind.

"You're smoking yourself retarded" she chuckled. "You really need to get off that shit." I kept on her, and eventually I convinced her to watch the documentary with me. At the end, she gave me a look that could kill and said, "Where's the bong?" No kidding, she dove in head first after watching the documentary. It is that powerful.

Marie and I became hemp activists within our social circles. She tried to turn her friends onto the truth about marijuana the same way I did her, with the documentary, and I tried to convince my friends to open their eyes, including many of my jiu-jitsu friends at Jean Jacques Machado's Academy. I made photocopies of chapters from The Emperor Wears No Clothes, stapled them together, and then passed them out to my coworkers at the strip club and to all my buddies at jiu-jitsu class. Most thought I had truly lost my mind, but a couple listened.

I ended up meeting Jack Herer at a few different hemp rallies over the years, and the one thing I remember most from our conversations was asking him why marijuana

2-3. Jack Herer, "The Emperor Wears No Clothes."
Available at: http://www.Jackherer.com

turbo-charges creativity. He told me that marijuana causes blood to flow to your head, just like Viagra sends blood flow to your meat-stick. He told me that's why your eyes get bloodshot. That totally made sense to me. If your lower back is injured, then a massage would do it good. Why? Because the massage breaks up the bullshit and sends it out with a rush of fresh blood. Blood is life. Blood is what vitamins, minerals, essential fatty acids, amino acids, and all other nutrients use as a vehicle to get to every body part to rescue and repair. So that was why every one of my senses was heightened when I was high. The more blood in the brain, the more it glows with life. Food tastes way better stoned, music sounds a hundred times better, and sex is on a whole other level. And you can't OD from it!

As my first few marijuana years passed, it was very intriguing to me how at first I didn't think I could do anything stoned except stay home and order food. But little by little, I started driving my car and even doing jiu-jitsu stoned. Whenever I hear newbie stoners say that they can't focus on anything while high, I always tell them my weed story. It's like the movie 'The Matrix.' In the first one, Neo is trippin' on the fact that he's in a computer program. It fucked up his game because the concept was too crazy for him to grasp. But by the third Matrix, he was kung fu fighting a hundred dudes in the sky. It was the same computer program in all three movies, it just took him a while to adjust to the altered state. And once you adjust to the increased amount of blood that's in your brain, you'll be able to perform at a whole new level. Think about it. Over 50% of NBA players smoke weed. Why do you think they don't test for weed in the NBA? Because they'll end up suspending most of the players in the league. But don't you need like some serious cardio to play professional basketball? …Exactly.

Here's another analogy that might make a little more sense to you. Let's say there's this author named Fedor. He's sixty-two years old, and he's written thirty-five books throughout his life, all on this super old vintage typewriter built in 1909. It's old as fuck, but to him, that's his baby. He's got that thing wired. He's been using that thing all his life and he's as fast on that thing as you can get. He's Floyd Mayweather on that fucking antique. But he doesn't know shit about computers. He's wouldn't even know how to turn a computer on. The man's a pimp daddy old skool author. But if he decided to write his new book on a laptop, all of a sudden his production would slow way the fuck down. It would take him a while before he could match the produc-

tion speed of the old typewriter. There's just way too much technology going on with the laptop for a lot of people to understand initially. Some might even get frustrated and break the fucking PC and go back to the old skool way. But if Fedor sticks it out and masters the ways of the mac, his overall writing output would quickly match that of the old writing method, and then soon go far beyond. That's just like smoking weed. Some people stick it out, learn how to use cannabis as a tool, and some freak out on it and run from it. And many people are way to brainwashed by the government propaganda to even think about doing it in the first place.

Stupid Stoners

And then there's a whole shit load of people who smoke weed but shouldn't. Remember, cannabis doesn't give you creativity; it just makes you more of what you already are. So if you're already dumb, please do humanity a favor and stay away from cannabis. I used to think it was the pot that made you stupid. I had a stoner friend while growing up who always said stupid ass shit, so I blamed the weed. Fuck, he was stupid. I was only fourteen and still seriously annoyed—imagine the idiocy. But I was wrong. Marijuana doesn't make you stupid, it makes stupid people feel they need to express their stupid thoughts. It makes you more of what you are, that's it. And there are a LOT of stupid stoners. A LOT.

Think about it. Smart kids want to do the right thing, and most of the time they do. If you tell a smart kid that pot makes you stupid, why wouldn't he believe you? Most children on this planet believe anything you tell them. That's why 90% of children believe in the same religion as their parents. And 90% of their parents believe in the same religion as their parents, and so on and on. We are all programmed monkeys. It's sooooo easy to brainwash children. Just because you're smart doesn't mean you're not brainwashed. We are all brainwashed, some more than others, and some WAY more.

Dumb kids don't care about doing the right thing. A lot of them don't care about their health because it makes them feel like they're rebelling. They're more inclined to do illegal shit, smoke cigarettes, drink underage, indulge in speed and cocaine, and maybe even use heroin. And since the government lumped a sacred, harmless, enlightening plant in with all that other stuff that can kill you, it shouldn't surprise you that dumb kids are smoking weed and giving intelligent smokers a bad name.

Ungrateful Stoners

I've noticed that there are a lot of stoners out there who don't understand what weed has done for them. Usually it's because they use other substances as well, such as alcohol, cocaine, or cigarettes. The mental and emotional benefits of cannabis gets muddled because of all the other shit they are taking.

This ungratefulness can also occur in stoners who have been smoking since an early age. They don't know what life without weed is like, so they take all the benefits for granted. For a guy like me who started smoking at twenty-eight, I definitely recognize the benefits. My personality was practically set in stone before I started smoking. It's kind of like I've lived two separate lives. In one life I lived with a mask that kept my soul in solitary confinement for nearly three decades, and in the other life my soul slowly dug its way out of the prison it had been sentenced to. I can't expect people who have been smoking since they were thirteen to understand the benefits because they have no clue what it is like to live without those benefits.

It's like being born into big money. If Paris Hilton entered a camel and goat semen-pulling tournament and won two million dollars, she probably wouldn't be that excited. It just wouldn't be that big of a deal. To her, money is probably "sooooo overrated!" She might not appreciate money at all because she's been raised with hundreds of millions of dollars. But if some thirty-year-old Brazilian lady from the ghettos of Rio, who is now cleaning houses in the states, won the animal-gripping competition, she would lose her fucking mind with joy. To her, that money would make such a gigantic difference in her life, and she would appreciate that two million dollars a billion times more than Paris. Same money, same competition, but two tremendously different reactions. Jack Herer is the most vocal, passionate marijuana activist that has ever lived, and he started smoking weed at thirty-five. Coincidence? I think not.

Joe's story

What about TV celebrity Joe Rogan? Did you know that he started smoking pot in his early thirties? He was one of the few people who actually listened to me back in the day when I would ramble about the wonders of marijuana. And since then, no one has talked about the benefits of cannabis on television and radio more than Joe. Not even Woody Harrelson. Woody doesn't even come close to Joe when it comes to spreading the word about weed through the media.

I met Joe at Jean Jacques back in '96 or '97. To me, he was just that actor dude who used to be on some obscure TV show that few people watched. At first we didn't really hang out, we would just say 'Hey, what's up dude?' to each other in the locker room. I actually ran into him at an old UFC, back when he first switched from Carlson Gracie to Jean Jacques' academy. It was the UFC where Frank Shamrock smashed Igor Zinoviev's collarbone with a big double leg slam. Joe was doing post fight interviews, and I was there with a friend. We spoke briefly, and the only thing I remember about our meeting is what he said to Vitor Belfort. Vitor was wearing a loud ass white sport coat and Joe said to me, "Check this out. I'm gonna go up to Vitor and ask him a fight question, and then I'm going to ask him why he's dressed up like the dude from Miami Vice. His English is so bad that he'll just keep talking about why he lost to Randy Couture." He actually did it, and I laughed my balls off. (On a side note, I choked a midget during that UFC, LIVE and on the telecast. I'm surprised no one has ever said anything to me about that.)

It wasn't until I showed up stoned as fuck one night with Darian at The Comedy Store in Hollywood that I found out that Joe was also a stand-up comedian. Now that the mechanics of comedy was making sense to me, Darian and I went to The Comedy Store quite often. When Joe hit the stage, I was like, "Oh shit! That's the actor dude from Jean Jacques!" Joe was funny as fuck; he had us busting up hard. Immediately I wondered if he smoked weed. But after he got off stage, I never had the chance to ask him. All I said was, "Dude, I had no idea you did comedy, you were funny as fuck!" He said thanks, and for a minute we talked some jiu-jitsu bullshit like, "How's your training going?"

Joe and I started becoming closer friends when he decided to take a jiu-jitsu lesson from me. I was just a purple belt at the time, but Joe was interested in my style of jiu-jitsu and my grappling philosophies. After the first lesson at his home, he was hooked on the Twister. He decided to take privates from me on a regular basis and concentrate on learning my style of jiu-jitsu. We hit it off right away because we had so fucking much in common, including our views on marriage, conspiracy theories, organized religion, and our love for MMA. But I was shocked that he didn't smoke weed. I thought to myself, 'Whoa! This mutha fucker is mad funny even without the creative turbo-charge that weed provides. If I can convince him to smoke weed, his comedy will for sure reach epic proportions!'

I was certain of this and made it a goal of mine. I was crazy eager to see how much his comedy would evolve and explode. I just hoped once I started talking about weed, he wouldn't think I was some crazy fuck like most of the people at Jean Jacques'. If I could enlighten him with weed, it would validate all my preaching at the academy. Then maybe they wouldn't think I was insane and, who knows, maybe some of them would finally open their eyes and get enlightened too. But I had to be careful with Joe because I didn't want to scare him away. I knew marijuana would provide him with new dimensions of comedy, and that would be undeniable proof that marijuana really is a powerful steroid for the imagination.

Well, Joe ended up listening to me and dove right in. We were in his car on our way to get something to eat, and right in the middle of my marijuana presentation, he pulled over and asked me to pull out the weed. I was like, "Dude, I don't think you should drive the first time you smoke weed. It took me a while before I started driving."

"Fuck it," he said. "Let's just do it!"

He took a couple of puffs and sped away. It was weird to me; he drove just fine and didn't have a bad trip or any negative feelings towards weed. However, it took him a while to fully understand its creative powers. For the first few weeks of his stoner days, he liked it, but he also thought I was giving weed way too much creative credit. I remember him telling me this about two hours after we smoked pot one night. Then I said to him, "Dude, ever since our first puff a couple of hours ago, we've been having one of the craziest, deepest conversations ever. We've been breaking down our lives, humanity, the cosmos, and the whole damn universe! Is this a coincidence?"

He didn't say anything. He just kind of nodded and a "Hhhhmmm" sneaked out of his body. Well, Joe slowly began to feel the power of marijuana, like I expected. His comedy went through the roof, skyrocketing into another galaxy. Listen to his first comedy CD that came out before weed invaded his mind. It was released in 2000 and is entitled 'I'm Gonna Be Dead Someday.' It's one of the funniest albums of its time, no doubt, but if you then listen to his comedy today, you'll see that it's a million times better and a billion times deeper. Before weed, he was the master of relationship jokes and sexual humor. He had that shit down just as good as any other comedian around. But now he has evolved into something very special. Today he's like some sort of new age philosopher who just so happens to make you laugh harder than any comedian that's ever lived. And I'm not just saying that because he's my best friend; he really is that good. He's actually unbelievably amazing, as a comedian and especially as a philosopher. I've toured the country with him quite a few times, and everyone on the comedy circuit knows that Joe is the next comic icon. They all know it—Chris Rock, Dave Chappelle, Andrew Dice Clay, all of them. They know. He is a rare, eclectic comedian that breaks down the building of the pyramids, the reality of the stars in our galaxy, the end of the world, human DNA, the war in the middle east, the catholic church, and of course plenty of cannabis humor. Joe is a monster now. By the time you read this, his Showtime Comedy Special 'Weed Made Me Smarter' should already be airing nationwide. Check your local listings and see for yourself. In the meantime, jump on www.myspace.com/talkingmonkey and see what he's up to right this minute. If you have an open mind, you will no doubt become a fan. He performs at many hemp rallies and medical marijuana benefits, as well as talks about marijuana on TV and radio. He's even hosted the High Times Music Awards in New York City. When it's all said and done, Joe will go down as the best comedian to ever live and one of the most important people in the movement to legalize marijuana, mark my words.

Be smart, smoke weed.

Foreword
By Joe Rogan

Have you ever been completely and totally wrong about something that you believed in with a passion? I believe that there are some very important, pivotal moments in our lives where we see things or learn things that force us to either rearrange our model of reality or deny the truth and slowly become delusional.

I've had several of these moments in my life that I navigated with varying levels of success, but for sure one of the most potent and profound of these moments was the day that Eddie Bravo introduced me to the wonders of the sacred plant known as cannabis. I'll never forget that day and the way it made me think. It was literally like an awakening. Like I woke up from a dream and found myself in a new world that I knew very little about. I realized just how flimsy my grasp on life really was. It caused me to reevaluate virtually every aspect of my life and make some serious changes.

I grew up competing in martial arts tournaments. For the most part I avoided alcohol, and I could count on one hand the number of times that I had smoked pot. I was very competitive, and I was also aware from personal experience that if I showed up for training hung over, I was probably going to get my ass kicked. Being an insecure teenager, fighting was scary enough, but doing something like drinking or getting high, which would make me fight below my abilities, just seemed retarded. So that was the main reason why I avoided pot. I always assumed that it had a similar impact on physical performance as alcohol, so there was no way I was letting that into my life.

While growing up I was painfully insecure most of the time, and an enormous portion of my self-esteem depended on my success in martial arts. It was the first thing that I ever did that made me feel like I was worth anything. It was the first thing I found that really made me stand out. My parents had separated when I was five, and my father stopped contacting me when I was seven. He's still alive, and to this day I haven't spoken a word with him; not a word since Christmas of my 8th year on the planet, which was over thirty years ago. That alone put a deep dent in my self-esteem.

My mom married my step dad when I was seven, and from that time until we settled in Boston when I was fourteen, we spent most of our time moving around the country. This lead to more insecurity because I never really had a group of stable friends. I kept changing schools, and I had to start over and over again trying to make new friends each time. To top it off, my stepfather was going to school this entire time, leaving my mom to bring home all the money. Needless to say, we were quite poor.

Martial arts was my first salvation. It gave me an opportunity to shine, to be something special, so I avoided anything that could fuck that up like the plague.

I think what worried me most was that I was really a loser, and that any success that I had would eventually fall apart. That was always the 'great fear' that I was running from, and I took every step needed to prevent that from becoming a reality.

I had a laundry list of all things associated with losers, and pot was firmly on that list, along with all the other drugs. People who were going nowhere in life smoked pot. I knew plenty of people who smoked, and at the time I considered them to be unambitious good for nothings.

Take a bath and get a job, you fucking hippie.

I carried this attitude right into adulthood. If you told me just six years ago that I would one day find myself writing a forward to a martial arts book, and in that book I was going to say that marijuana changed my life, I would have told you that you were out of your fucking mind.

But it did, and here I am.

It all started for me when I began hanging out with Eddie. I knew him from jiu-jitsu class, and most people thought of him as this wild dude that had a crazy submission game. We hung around a couple times, and he seemed like a really intelligent, interesting guy. We talked about and agreed on a lot of subjects, including religion, politics, the nature of people, the cosmos—all kinds of shit. So when he told me that pot was the reason why he was so creative, I was really shocked. He was a hard worker and very ambitious, both with his jiu-jitsu and his music. I couldn't believe he was telling me that the reason he got so good at both those things was because he was a pothead?

I couldn't believe it, but I could recognize that if he happened to be right, it was something pretty huge. "Fuck it, I'll try it out," was basically what I said. I figured if he was wrong, no big deal. I get high and feel like shit in the morning—lesson learned. But if he was right… if he really had let me in on this incredible secret that could change the way I looked at everything… well, that HAD to be worth a chance.

I can still remember the way it hit me that first day. I think it was probably the only time in my life that I had smoked pot without drinking alcohol, except for maybe one or two times as a teenager. I can still clearly remember the flood of new thoughts and ideas pouring into my brain. It was like someone opened up a valve to a new reservoir of consciousness. I couldn't fucking believe it. Eddie was right.

Slowly pot worked its way into my life. It wasn't a completely smooth process; at first it used to make me really paranoid. It forced me to think about all these things that I was subconsciously aware of, but that my ego shielded me from in everyday life. Several times I was really jolted by it, and I would have waves where I didn't want to smoke it anymore because I didn't like the uncomfortable feeling brought on by the forced awareness. It took me a while to get comfortable with it, but Eddie helped me through this

phase by explaining to me that this was natural, and that the weirdness I experienced was just my ego fighting my awakening. I had trusted him to try it, so I trusted that he was right about getting used to it.

Take a deep breath, and slowly embrace the effects of the red pill.

Over time I watched my personality evolve. I started to become nicer to people and more relaxed. I started writing much, much more than before, and the thoughts that came out were occasionally so alien to what my mind had previously produced that it was like someone else was writing for me, and I was channeling it. I still feel like that sometimes, six years later. It completely changed my comedy. So much so that I view my comedy career in two phases; pre-weed and post-weed. I became a completely different comic.

Pre-weed I was just doing stuff that I thought would work. Some of it I thought was funny, but there was a lot of shit that I was doing onstage only because it got laughs. However, post-weed my act evolved over the course of several years into an extension of my life's philosophy. As my personal thoughts and ideas grew, my onstage material went deeper and deeper. I went from doing mostly sex jokes to talking about what I was really thinking about; life, death, religion, genetics, animal instincts, and ultimately the universe itself. Weed completely revamped my stand-up comedy career. It gave me a newfound appreciation and enthusiasm for the art form. To this day I never write without it, and I very, very rarely go onstage without first getting high.

Nowadays, I'm frequently called upon to give interviews about pot. I perform regularly at medical marijuana benefits in LA, and I enthusiastically tell anyone who asks about the effect marijuana has had on me. One of the things that Eddie and I have talked about a lot is how weird it is that more people don't give weed the credit it deserves when it comes to influencing and enhancing their art. I think the propaganda that the government distributed in the 30's was so potent and pervasive that even some of the potheads of today are affected by it to a certain extent. They'll recite the medicinal uses for it, and the industrial uses for hemp fiber, but rarely do you hear people giving credit to it for the evolution of their thoughts and ideas. A part of this probably has to do with the fact that many stoners have smoked pot for a good portion of their life, and they don't realize the full effect it's had on them. Because I didn't start using cannabis until I was in my thirties, I'm very, very aware of the magical qualities it possesses, and the incredible effect it's had on me. I was already a grown man with a fully formed personality and a successful career when I first got turned onto it, and I think that's why I appreciate it in a different way than the average pothead.

What's really amazing is that it's illegal. In a country where cigarettes kill 400,000 people each and every year, marijuana has killed zero. A hundred and fifty people die each year from coconuts falling on their heads, and pot kills zero. Prescription drugs kill over 100,000 each year, including a lot of drugs that would be completely unnecessary if pot was legal, and who knows how many are killed by alcohol, especially when you factor in not just alcohol overdoses, but drunk driving accidents, suicide, and booze inspired violence.

All the while, marijuana remains harmless. It's a plant that grows naturally, all over the world. It kills no one, it's got dozens of medicinal uses, it acts as a turbocharger for your imagination, and yet it can get you locked up in a cage if you're caught with it. Seriously, is that not some of the craziest shit you've ever heard in your fucking life? Before you answer that question, I think perhaps you should smoke a joint and really think about it.

That's my story, and I hope it inspires some of you out there to ask some questions of your own, review your life, and possibly change the path of your own story. I wish you the best of luck, and I thank you for your time.

-Joe Rogan

Introduction

Training jiu-jitsu with a gi is like riding a crotch rocket through a residential neighborhood. It's fun, no doubt about it. But training jiu-jitsu without the gi is like taking that same crotch rocket out onto the freeway. It's faster. There is less stalling. You've got to slow down every once in a while for traffic, but mostly you're in fifth gear hauling ass. This is the style of jiu-jitsu that I enjoy.

Latching onto an opponent's collar or sleeve to set up submissions has never been my cup of tea, so shortly after I started rolling, I began developing a style of jiu-jitsu that didn't depend upon the gi. I created submissions that were set up using over-hooks and under-hooks. I designed control positions that allow you to break an opponent down into your guard and then keep him tied up in the clinch. If one of my innovations didn't work, I either fixed it or threw it out. There were many throw outs. After a decade of experimenting and building, I had created a system of jiu-jitsu designed specifically for the street, mixed martial arts competition, and no-gi grappling tournaments.

I was quite pleased with this creation, but stepping away from tradition had labeled me as a traitor in many circles. A large number of Brazilian Jiu-Jitsu instructors held the gi in such high regard that they didn't even consider my system of grappling jiu-jitsu. I honestly couldn't see what the fuss was all about. Why were they so attached to the uniform they wore during training? Whether you're wearing a gi or not, an arm bar is still an arm bar. Passing the guard is still passing the guard. It's the same strategy; you just

have different methods to reach the same end. I never boasted that my system was superior—my only claim was that it worked better in situations where uniforms were not involved, such as in MMA and no-gi grappling tournaments. I didn't feel as though I was hanging out on a limb with this statement. I figured anyone who gave it a decent amount of thought would realize that I was right. If the majority of your set-ups require you to grab hold of an opponent's gi, and suddenly you're going up against an opponent who isn't wearing a gi, what are you going to do? Unless you've learned how to utilize over-hooks and under-hooks, all your set-ups just went flying straight out the window.

I was quite vocal about my opinions while commentating for the King of the Cage, a popular MMA event. Most of the jiu-jitsu practitioners who listened to me on air considered me certifiably insane, so I decided to prove the effectiveness of my system in 2003 by entering Abu Dhabi, the largest and most respected no-gi jiu-jitsu tournament in the world. I'm quite sure those who disliked my philosophy and training methods wanted me to suffer horrible defeat, and I'm equally as sure that they felt a fair amount of frustration when I used my no-gi style to defeat Royler Gracie, the most respected member of the legendary Gracie family. I didn't expect the gi lovers to jump for joy, but I truly thought that they would admit I was onto something. Instead they did their best to sweep my victory under the rug. It was the largest upset in Abu Dhabi history, and they simply ignored it.

I figured the American jiu-jitsu press would at least give me some props in the magazines, but that never happened either. Apparently the majority of reporters working for the jiu-jitsu media were still clinging to the gi as well. I believe this to be true because the story of the American who traveled down to Brazil and beat the pride and joy of the Gracie family never appeared in the jiu-jitsu magazines. I wasn't asking for a cover shot, but a small article in the back would have been nice. Instead they offered shots of me being jacked by Leo Vieira in the semi-finals. I'm totally cool with that, but at least accompany it with a shot of me defeating Royler. Call me crazy, but I thought the American jiu-jitsu media would hype up the victory. I thought they would be proud that one of their boys beat the top dog.

The whole situation made me take a hard look at the politics surrounding jiu-jitsu, and it didn't take long for things to become crystal clear. All I had to do was pretend that the hundreds of jiu-jitsu instructors in the United States who made a living teaching students how to grapple with a gi were Volkswagen mechanics. They didn't have a clue about how to work on Fords, but they could fix the hell out of a Volkswagen. I was the guy out there selling Fords. Of course they weren't going to support me. The more people I convinced to buy a Ford, the fewer Volkswagen would be sold. And the fewer Volkswagens sold, the fewer cars they would have to work on. It affected their livelihood. So how could I expect them to acknowledge the fact that I took my Ford out onto the track and whopped the best Volkswagen on the market? I couldn't. It would be just as ridiculous to think that Volkswagen magazine would publish an article on the race. After all, the majority of their writers were Volkswagen mechanics. Which one of them would be willing to write such an article?

I understood the politics, but it still didn't seem right. In the early 90's jiu-jitsu practitioners had ridiculed the eastern martial artists for following tradition. The Brazilian Jiu-Jitsu motto was, 'Do what works,' but now that jiu-jitsu had the popularity and clout, the motto had changed. It had become, 'Brazilian Jiu-Jitsu has made all the advancements possible in the martial arts. The evolution is complete.'

This was far from the truth. Squashing the fact that it's more beneficial to train without a gi for MMA competition might benefit the instructors, but it hurt students who wanted to reach their goal of becoming fighters. Was it right for students to be brainwashed? Was it right for them to face expulsion if they should talk about training without a gi? I thought not.

Eddie Bravo & Royler Gracie
Photo by Howard Liu

With mixed martial arts and no-gi grappling growing more popular by the day, I figured a lot of people desired to learn a form of jiu-jitsu that didn't depend upon the gi. Specializing in this type of grappling, I decided to open an academy in Hollywood, California. I had hoped that 10th Planet Jiu-Jitsu would become a haven for grapplers who wished to step away from tradition and continue the evolution of the sport, and that's just what it became. The amount of people who walked through my academy doors was shocking. It let me know I was truly onto something. The only thing that caught me by surprise was the amount of controversy my school stirred up in the jiu-jitsu community.

A miniature war sparked up between those who trained jiu-jitsu with a gi and those who didn't. There was a lot of trash talked about my Rubber Guard and anyone who used it. It got so heated that I decided to write a book on the controversy, put my whole system out there and let people decide for themselves what worked and what didn't. I wanted to show people that there was another path, not just the one that had been drilled into their heads by instructors and the martial arts media. I wanted to let them know that if I could stray from the beaten path and defeat a legend like Royler Gracie, anyone could do it.

The problem was I didn't have the slightest clue about how to get a book deal. I ended up talking with my instructor Jean Jacques, who had published several highly successful books on the sport. It turned out that his ghostwriter, the guy who put the book projects together, was a student of Royler Gracie and an avid believer in the gi. It quickly dawned on me that approaching the guy to do a book on my no-gi style probably wouldn't produce the most pleasant conversation. It most certainly wouldn't produce a book deal.

I wasn't willing to give up. There were people on the internet asking me to do a DVD, but I was still hooked on the book idea. You can get much more descriptive in a book, break down the philosophy behind each move. Students could also take a book wherever they wanted. If they wished to learn a new jiu-jitsu move while sitting on the crapper, they didn't have to drag a television in there with them.

Continuing my hunt, I called Turi Altavilla, a friend I had met while working with the King of the Cage organization. He had since moved onto the PRIDE Fighting Championships, and I thought he might have some contacts in the book world. He told me he would get back to me. The very next day, I was contacted out of the blue by a writer named Erich Krauss. He had been contracted by McGraw Hill, one of the big New York publishing houses, to do a book on the sport of jiu-jitsu. Apparently McGraw Hill had noticed some of the smaller publishing houses making big cash on these jiu-jitsu books, and they decided to get a piece of the pie. Krauss had talked with Larry Goldberg, owner of Boxinginsider.com, and Larry had put him in touch with me. I saw the whole thing as fate. I was also extremely pumped by the offer sitting on my plate. None of the other jiu-jitsu books on the market had been published by one of the big boys. I was convinced that I would get my message out in a big way.

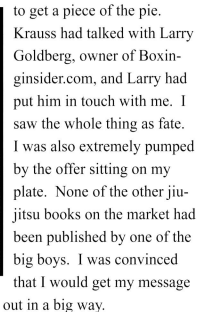

When Turi called me back a couple of days later to give me his contacts and I told him that I already had a book deal, he couldn't believe it. Neither could I.

My enthusiasm started to fade as restrictions poured in. I found out that McGraw Hill planned to do the photos in black and white, and we were limited on the number of photos we could include. The topic of cannabis arose—I didn't feel the publisher would be comfortable with me talking about how pot had fueled my jiu-jitsu game. I didn't even have control over the title. It was great that I had been picked up by McGraw Hill, but I started to think that a smaller house might have been better. I looked forward less and less to my title being on the shelves.

They ended up calling it *Jiu-Jitsu Unleashed*, and despite all the restrictions placed upon the book and almost no marketing campaign to speak of, it did quite well. In fact, it did so well the publishing house offered me a large advance to do a second book. I told them I would do it, but I had to have total control. They informed me that they simply didn't do that with authors. What they did do was double my advance money. It was quite a sum for a guy who lives off teaching jiu-jitsu, but both Krauss and I felt that we needed total control over this one. If we were going to do another book, this one focusing on the Rubber Guard, it couldn't just scratch the surface of my system. It had to dive deep.

Showing a hundred different submissions wasn't enough; we had to get in-depth with each of the Rubber Guard positions, talk strategy. We wanted to give the reader tricks to get around blockades, as well show them how to combine their newfound submissions, sweeps, escapes, and transitions into combinations to increase their effectiveness. We had to give them ways to deal with the stack, offer them techniques to stop an opponent from picking them up and slamming them back down, and show them how to alter their guard game when competing in MMA. There were more than a hundred Rubber Guard techniques we wanted to lay out, but merely throwing them down on paper

Compella & The Twister

would mean little unless we presented the massive, intricate web that interlocks every technique, and then teach the reader how to move about that web to accomplish various goals. It was a tall order we didn't feel our former publisher would be up for tackling.

To deal with our dilemma of where to go to get our book deal, Krauss started calling all the best people he had worked with in the publishing industry over the years. Apparently, all the publishing houses had their eyes locked on the sport of mixed martial arts. With the UFC getting more and more popular every day with its reality television show, it wasn't hard to convince editors and the like that a jiu-jitsu book geared directly toward the MMA crowd would sell big time. After several meetings, Victory Belt was born, a publishing house dedicated to putting out top-of-the-line books on the sport of the future. They told me I had control over the title. I had control over the number of pictures. They wouldn't edit out anything I wanted to say, including my opinions on marijuana. And I had a lot of things I wanted to say about pot. The problem was I had a lot of techniques and strategy I needed to cover first. After all the photo shoots and interviews, I realized that there might not be any room left for putting in my personal stories. Hell, there wouldn't even be enough room for my entire jiu-jitsu game. This posed another dilemma, but Victory Belt quickly came back with a solution—lets do two books. The first one would be dedicated exclusively to the Rubber Guard, which is the book you are now holding. The second one would be dedicated to Twister Side Control, the mount, the back, and all the other positions other than those of the guard. It would also contain my personal stories, beliefs, and feelings on marijuana. I thought it was a grand idea.

The one thing I made sure to touch upon in both books were all the questions people had shot by me over the years concerning my game. To get an even better idea of what people wanted to learn, I posted a questionnaire on the internet. Jiu-jitsu practitioners from around the world came back with more than a hundred questions, the answers to which I tried to weave into the narrative of the books. However, a lot of the questions I received still had to do with the gi vs. no-gi controversy. Basically, if someone eventually wants to fight in MMA or compete in no-gi grappling tournaments, should they train with a gi or without one? I wanted to answer that question to the best of my ability, but truthfully I was getting tired of hearing about it. It was getting ridiculous.

Only in the sport of jiu-jitsu do you hear such foolishness. In all my years, I have never heard a Greco Roman wrestler ask if he should train judo in order to get good at Greco Roman. Both sports have the same goal, to throw your opponent, but they are vastly different because in one the competitors wear a gi and in the other they don't. Why learn how to throw an opponent utilizing the gi if none of your opponents will be wearing a gi? It doesn't make sense. And if it did make sense, then every four years the judo guys would win the Olympic gold metal in Greco Roman wrestling. The last time I checked, that wasn't the case.

It's the exact same thing with sport jiu-jitsu and MMA fighting. If you find yourself lying on your back, you have the same goal—get a sweep or finish your opponent off your back. When you're on top you have the same goal—pass your opponent's guard, and then claim the mount position or take your opponent's back. It's the exact same strategy, but the grips are totally different. One utilizes over-hooks and under-hooks, and the other utilizes the gi. The way you gain control of your opponent is so important that it makes traditional Brazilian Jiu-Jitsu and no-gi grappling two separate sports, just like Greco Roman wrestling and judo. You never hear a Greco Roman coach tell his students that in order for them to reach their full potential they must first study judo. You just don't hear it. So then why do we hear jiu-jitsu instructors saying that in order to get good at no-gi grappling you must first train with the gi?

I haven't a clue. All I can suggest at this point is for you to sit back and ask yourself what you want to accomplish. If you want to compete in traditional jiu-jitsu competition, by all means you should train with a gi. If you want to compete in no-gi grappling tournaments such as Abu Dhabi or compete in mixed martial arts, train without a gi. Study my system.

I realize for a lot of people taking the gi off can be difficult. In addition to being loyal to their instructors, they also don't want to start over in a new sport. It can be a humbling experience getting beat by a guy with less experience, but it's better than closing your eyes to the truth and then getting beat down in the ring or cage because you didn't train to control your opponent with over-hooks and under-hooks.

I've spelled it out like this a thousand times, yet the controversy carries on. Not long ago I realized that I could talk for a hundred years and still I wouldn't make any headway. I might convince a few people new to the sport who hadn't already fallen under an instructor's influence, but those who currently lived by the gi would continue to do so. They would never convince me to train with a gi, and I would never convince them to train without one. At that point I realized that it was probably best to let people make up their own minds. Instead of preaching, I posted a hypothetical question on the internet that breaks down the whole controversy. If someone read the entire question, thought about it, and decided that my perception was wrong, so be it. I just wanted to get peoples' minds whirling, get them to consider all the facts before making a decision.

The No-gi Hypothetical Question

Let's pretend this year Royler Gracie opened two new schools in Los Angeles on the same day. One in Compton, and one in East Los Angeles.

All students from both schools are 100% inexperienced.

The East LA school is strictly a gi school with intentions of producing multiple Mundial champions.

The Compton school is a pure no-gi school with intentions of producing Abu Dhabi and Grapplers Quest champions.

Royler spends equal time at both schools.

Within eight years, a student from the East LA school shows tremendous promise. His name is Panchito Manuelo Gonzalez Fernandez, but due to time constraints, we will call him Pancho. He's collar choking everyone, from the Copa Pacifca to Joe Moriera's Nationals. He's also the leader of the LA street gang "18th Street", and claims to have choked out hundreds of gang rivals (apparently Raider jerseys are ideal for choking).

This guy is ferocious! He's 235 pounds and very tall for a Mexican. On his back he even has a giant tattoo of Jesus dressed in a Gameness Gi and nailed to the cross.

After choking everyone he faced unconscious at the Pan Ams a year later (4 Clocks and 3 Ezikiels), Royler is forced to give Pancho his black belt. A phenom is born.

Meanwhile over at the Compton no-gi school, nine years has also produced a monster, LeTron Jackson. Tron, as his dogs know him, has developed a sick Rear Naked Choke and is also known for his dangerous guard (brutha's got some long ass lizzeggs).

Tron is 55 and 2 in no-gi competition, with 52 of his wins coming by way of submission. Not bad considering his first loss came at the hands of a grappling legend, Beast Ozinga from 10TH PLANET JIU JIT-SU, and his second loss was due to his baby's momma trippin' at the tourney, causing Tron to lose focus.

Tron has become a serious grappling pimp, choking out bitches til six in the morn.

With Tron sweeping the ADCC trials at the end of the ninth year, he enters the Abu Dhabi Submission Wrestling Tournament the heavyweight favorite.

The tenth year of Royler's LA schools was HUGE!

Pancho took the gold at the 2014 Mundials, despite losing four homies the week before in a drive-by shooting.

And Tron also added to Royler's gold medal collection by taking first place at ADCC 2014.

Royler has once again proven to be one the best BJJ instructors in the world, gi AND no-gi.

But as Pancho and Tron's popularity rises, so does their already incredible egos, and within months they go from Gracie teammates to arch rivals.

This is how it went down:

Pancho called Tron a "Myate" (Spanish for the N word) in an interview with Grappling Magazine. Apparently Tron claimed to be Royler's number one student on a popular grappling message board on the internet, and that made Pancho furious.

"Shhhheeeetttt, of muthafuckin' course I'm Royler's number one dog, you betta axe somebody!" -Tron

"Number one? Fuck that myate, holmes. He doesn't even know real jiu-jitsu, esse. He's never worn a gi, vatto. Fuckin' myate!" -Pancho

Royler immediately kicks Pancho out of the Gracie Association for the racial slurs and challenges Pancho to a no time limit/no points/NO-GI match against Tron.

Pancho accepts, and Tron vows to make Pancho eat a refried shit burrito.

NOW HERE IS THE MILLION DOLLAR QUESTION:

Based on the info I gave you about these fighters, if you had to bet everything you had on this match, who would you chose? Pancho or Trizzon?

Finding the Right Guard

If you purchased this book in the hopes of acquiring a guard game that will be successful one hundred percent of the time, you will be disappointed. No guard system works a hundred percent of the time. To realize this all you have to do is watch a dozen or so MMA matches. Add up all the times the fights end up in the guard, and then count the number of times the fighters on bottom manage to finish their opponents. The percentages are extremely low. A part of the reason is because people are learning phenomenal guard defense, and an even larger part of it is because no one is trying anything different from the guard.

The type of guard most fighters play in MMA is double wrist control. If you are under the assumption that holding onto your opponent's wrists is a good strategy, again I ask you to examine an MMA bout that goes to the guard. Count the times the opponent on bottom gets punched. Count the times he is successful with his submissions. Occasionally he'll catch a wild Triangle, but the percentages are very low. I developed the Rubber Guard not because I think it looks cool, but rather because I'm trying to improve upon those percentages.

I know for a fact that the Rubber Guard will make your guard game more lethal. I know this because it's the only guard system that allows you to keep your opponent broken down into the clinch and yet still have one free arm to work for submissions, transitions, and escapes. This just so happens to translate very well to MMA and Abu Dhabi style grappling. Take two boxers for example—do they hit each other more often when they are in punching range or when they are in the clinch? Not only do they get hit less often while tied up in the clinch, they also get hit with less powerful shots. The same principles apply to the guard.

When you play the Rubber Guard, which allows you to tie your opponent up in the clinch, you get hit less often than you do when playing double wrist control, which keeps your opponent on the outside. You also get hit with a lot weaker punches.

When the Rubber Guard is played right, you will never have to hug your opponent and wait for the referee to break you apart. You will never have to risk taking these huge shots while hunting for a submission. The Rubber Guard allows you to maintain a defensive posture and still press the fight.

It's not an easy system to master; you have to dedicate some serious hours to its development over the course of several years, but you would have to do that with any guard system. If you want to be effective fighting off your back, it takes work.

In my mind, sticking with a system that works a low percentage of the time is not an option. If a sport isn't constantly evolving, then it's dying. Football is always moving forward. Read the professional playbook from the sixties and compare it to the plays you see today. The west coast offense made huge refinements in the 80's, and today teams are combining those refinements with the original book to create these insane hybrid plays. Basketball too is evolving. Ten years ago it was just Michael Jordan and a couple of others doing this crazy shit. They showed the other players what was actually possible, and now a whole generation is doing insane passes and slams. If you're not constantly changing your jiu-jitsu game, coming up with new and more effective set-ups, then you're going to get left behind.

Gi Pants

When both you and your grappling partner are wearing shorts and nothing else, the sweat factor is huge. In just a matter of minutes it can become like a hot-oil wrestling match. To cut down on all the slipping and sliding, I wear gi pants. It makes my overall guard game forty percent more effective, and it makes me fifty percent more effective with the Lockdown. In case my pants slide up my leg, I wear a support bandage over my calves called Tubigrip, which helps me lock in Omaplatas, Triangles, and Arm Bars. I also wear an ankle sleeve that adds gripping power to my foot and helps keep the Lockdown tight.

This is the ensemble that I put on each and every time I train. I know it might sound a little strange coming from a no-gi advocate, but if given some thought, you will realize that the jacket is what the gi game depends upon, not the pants. You can grab the collar or sleeve of your opponent's gi top and use that grip to set up a submission or sweep. You can latch onto your opponent's belt and set up submissions and sweeps as well. You can even use your opponent's collar to choke him unconscious. The gi top is everything in traditional Brazilian Jiu-Jitsu.

You can't use gi pants to help set up a submission, but they help a great deal to cut down on some of the slipping and sliding. My instructor Jean Jacques convinced me to wear shorts in the 2003 Abu Dhabi trials. Although I won, I felt there was too much slippage going on. When I went up against with Royler down in Brazil, I wore shorts with knee sleeves, but I still felt there was too much slippage. I went back to the pants, and then I added Tubigrip and ankle sleeves into the mix. Now I feel insecure without them.

With both my half guard and Rubber Guard games dependant upon friction, I rely heavily upon the gi pants. Without the pants you can still play the Rubber Guard, but your percentages will inevitably go down. Your opponent will be able to slip out of Mission Control a lot easier. He will be able to pull out of the Lockdown a lot easier. You can still benefit from my system if you decide not to wear pants, but you won't be able to make the most out of it.

It truly surprises me that more people don't train with just the pants. Brazilian Jiu-Jitsu practitioners who worship the gi wear the entire uniform or just shorts. MMA fighters who strictly do no-gi grappling usually refuse to wear anything but shorts. It wouldn't be a large step for the traditional guys to strip off their gi tops, and it wouldn't be a major leap for the MMA guys to exchange their shorts for pants. After all, most gi pants are just slightly longer than the grappling shorts that reach down to the knees. That extra few inches of fabric could mean landing a submission or preventing an opponent from slipping out of your guard.

However, there are a few downsides to wearing pants. The primary downside is that it's harder to defend against leg locks. This is particularly true if you're playing double wrist control because it's relatively easy for your opponent to access your legs. But if you're playing the Rubber Guard, your opponent will be trapped in the clinch the majority of the time. He won't have an opportunity to get you in a leg lock in the first place. And if he does manage to get you in a leg lock, the deciding factor as to whether or not he gets the submission doesn't always come down to what you are wearing. There are guys out there so proficient with leg locks that they can submit you even when you're wearing shorts.

The other downside to wearing pants is that your opponent can use them to help him execute a sweep or pass your guard. This too won't be much of a factor once you get good at breaking your opponent's grips. Every time an opponent grabs your pants, you simply chop their grips with the inside of your forearm to break them apart. It's pretty straightforward and simple.

Although there are a few negatives that go along with wearing pants, I would much rather sacrifice a little defense for a lot more offense. I would rather have a big ass Rambo machine gun and a small shield than a big shield and a twenty-two. I'm not saying either way is right or wrong. It's just my style.

How to Use This Book

This book is essentially a road map for the Rubber Guard. I've laid out my entire half guard game, my entire butterfly guard game, and my entire Rubber Guard game. These systems are linked together to form a greater system, and if you skip over one, your game will be incomplete. Only after you have a grasp of each position and understand how these positions work together will you develop the clear-cut direction so many jiu-jitsu practitioners are lacking in their guard game.

The Rubber Guard starts with breaking your opponent down into your guard and then keeping him tied up in the clinch with a position called Mission Control. From Mission Control there is a distinct route you will travel. If you can catch your opponent with a submission while traveling along your path, it's all the better. But if you can't get a submission because his defenses are sharp, you still have direction. You understand the tasks you must complete to reach the next control position, and the one after that. You work up the control position ladder one rung at a time until you trap your opponent in what I like to call a dead zone, which is a control position so dominant you can taste the submission.

To become proficient with the Rubber Guard, you must not only commit that main path to memory, but you must also learn the alternate routes I have laid out in the following pages. Achieve that and few blockades can stand in your way. If your opponent counters a butterfly guard sweep by posting his arm, you can use his new positioning to transition into the Pyramid control position. If he attempts to roll out of an Oma-plata submission when you have him in the Jiu-Claw control position, you can use his escape to transition into Twister Side Control. The goal of this book is to not only lay out as many of these scenario based options as possible, but to also help you to acquire the tools and creativity to come up with options of your own.

After you have gotten a handle on the control positions, the submissions available from each of the control positions, and how to transition back and forth between the control positions to shatter your opponent's defense, the next step toward mastering the Rubber Guard is developing speed. If your opponent has never before seen the Rubber Guard, you will most likely be  able to submit him with your unorthodox submissions. But if he has been doing his homework like many jiu-jitsu practitioners, he will know exactly where you want to head and when. To defeat such opponents, you must be able to climb the next rung of the ladder before he can counter that step.

The majority of my students know all the Rubber Guard submissions, counters, escapes, and transitions like the back of their hand. When two of them climb onto the mat to roll, the victor is usually the one who manages to get one step ahead on 'the path'. While his opponent is still defending his previous submission attempt or transition, he is already moving onto the next.

In the following pages I have laid out all the tools you will need to reach such a level. To become a master, all you need to invest is lots of practice and dedication.

The reason the book starts with the half guard is because you'll probably spend a good deal of time there in the beginning. Until you nail down the control positions of the Rubber Guard—really develop your technique through countless hours and repetitions—expect your opponents to have a relatively easy time passing your guard. As your opponent executes his pass, you'll usually be able to capture him in your half guard. If you study the book from cover to cover, you will not be timid about working from this position. Because my entire guard game is linked together, you will have clear direction in the half guard as well. You'll know exactly where to go at all times. You will also be developing the squeezing power and endurance needed to have an effective Rubber Guard. If you find your opponents routinely passing your guard completely, claiming the mount or side control, then you should refer to the 'Escaping Back to Guard' section at the end of the book.

Just take things slow and progressively move upward through each control position. Before you know it, you'll be breaking your opponents down into the clinch while everyone else is still playing double wrist control. You will have direction while everyone else is throwing up random submission attempts. You will have a guard system that works a larger percentage of the time.

Part One

STRETCHING

Introduction to Stretching

Over the years I've noticed that jiu-jitsu students tend to look at stretching differently than students of kickboxing or karate. If a guy walks into a kickboxing school for the first time and comes to the sudden realization that he can't kick someone to the head, he doesn't write the sport off. He doesn't think that anyone who can kick to the head is some sort of genetic freak. What usually goes through his mind is, "Man, if I want to kick someone to the head, I've got to stretch."

It seems like a natural thought process, but so often in jiu-jitsu that thought process doesn't occur. When a new student sees something like the Rubber Guard, sees positions that require a certain amount of flexibility, they instantly think, "Oh man, you have to be born flexible to pull off those kind of freaky moves." Such a statement is completely untrue. Just like being able to pull off a head kick in karate, you have to stretch to effectively pull off control positions like those in the Rubber Guard. It's all right if you're not super flexible your first day experimenting with Rubber Guard techniques, but you've got to delegate time out of every day to stretching so three or four months down the road the majority of techniques in this book will be available to you.

You should stretch before and after every practice. You should stretch while you're watching TV, hanging out with your girlfriend, or just chilling at work. I constantly sit in crazy positions when I'm lounging to increase my flexibility. Just sitting cross-legged stretches out your knees and hips, which is perfect for jiu-jitsu. I've had guys come to my school who couldn't come close to touching their knees to the mat in the butterfly stretch position, and then just three or four months later they could get their knees all the way

down. The key is being patient and sticking with your stretching routine. The Rubber Guard techniques that require the most flexibility are a lot easier to master than most people imagine.

Included in the upcoming section are also my favorite yoga stretches. I've had chronic back problems for fifteen years, and training jiu-jitsu has only made them worse. Playing guard is particularly painful. When I first started rolling I did everything I could think of to alleviate the pain. I tried acupuncture, and that didn't work. I tried deep-tissue massage, and that didn't work. I tried to baby my lower back by maintaining good posture and bending over the right way, and that still didn't help. Then one day a student of mine named Ralf, who happened to be an former German track star, showed me a handful of yoga exercises that I could do before training. They helped strengthen all the muscles and supporting muscles in my back and got blood pumping to the area. After a few weeks, I suffered considerably less pain while my back was getting smashed and twisted and torqued in the guard.

If you plan on training a significant amount of jiu-jitsu, it is also beneficial to schedule regular appointments with a chiropractor. When I can, I go twice a week to see Dr. Peter Goldman, who also happens to be BJ Penn's chiropractor. With his adjustments and the constant stretching, my back gives me a lot less problems.

In addition to trying out some of the stretches I have included, you should also experiment with stretching exercises of your own. If you are unsure of what stretches to do, there are many excellent books on this subject. I could have included a hundred basic stretches in the upcoming pages, but it would only be repeating what is already out there.

Butterfly Stretch

The butterfly stretch should be the bread and butter of all jiu-jitsu stretching routines because it increases the flexibility of your hips, knees, and groin. The more flexible you are in these areas, the more options you will have to attack and defend while playing guard. In this exercise, it is important that you apply downward pressure to your knees with either your hands or elbows to get the most out of the stretch, but it is equally as important not to overstep your limitations. Tearing a muscle can force you off the mat for weeks or even months. Generally you should hold this stretch for at least thirty seconds, shake your legs out for a few moments, and then repeat until your hips, knees, and groin feel loose and relaxed.

Sitting on the mat with my back straight, I place the bottom of my feet together and pull my heels toward my groin. To get the most out of the stretch, I set my hands on my knees and press down. Don't get discouraged if this is as low as you can go. If you practice this stretch at the beginning of every practice, you WILL get more flexible.

As my hips and groin loosen, I apply additional downward pressure on my knees to move them closer to the mat. It is important to maintain good posture as you do this, as well as make sure your heels don't slide away from your groin.

Because I've spent so much time stretching and rolling, I am able to press my knees to the mat without discomfort. To increase the stretching pressure, I lean slightly forward.

Removing my hands from my knees, I stretch my arms forward. Notice how I am keeping my head up, eyes forward, and my back straight. If your knees pop up as you reach forward, return to the previous position until you acquire the proper flexibility.

I take this stretch to its limit by keeping my heels tucked to my groin, pinning my hips and knees to the mat, and dropping my torso down onto my feet. Achieving this position can sometimes take years, so it is important that you go at your own pace and not try to force it.

Hamstring Stretch

Although this stretch is designed to increase the flexibility of your hamstrings, it also loosens up your obliques and lower back. It is important that you strive to grab your toes, but at the same time you always want to keep your extended leg flat on the mat. If your knee pops up, give up on your toes for the time being and latch onto your shin. In time, your foot will be within reach.

Tucking my left heel into my groin, I reach my left arm over my head with my thumb pointing down. Then I grab the toes of my right foot with my right hand. If you can't reach your toes without elevating your right knee, you are most likely overstepping your limitations. Start by latching onto your knee with your right hand, and then slowly crawl your hand down your leg until you can reach your toes.

Step Over Hip Stretch

Having flexible hips is key to playing every guard—closed, open, butterfly, and Rubber. Not only does it allow you to move into and out of the guard easier, but it also gives you the versatility to use your arms and legs together. Mission Control is a perfect example. Instead of using both arms and legs to control your opponent in your guard, you control him by throwing a leg over his shoulder and then securing it in place by grabbing your foot with one hand. This not only keeps your opponent's posture down, but it also frees up your other hand and allows you to hunt for a submission. But in order to make the most out of positions like Mission Control, you must develop flexible hips. That flexibility will also help you in other positions, including the mount and side control. The more flexible your hips become, the more options open up. For these reasons, the stretch below should be done as often as possible.

While in the sitting position, I coil my left heel toward my right buttocks. I then place my right foot over my left leg, keeping my knee snug to my body. To add additional pressure to the stretch, I wrap my left arm around my right knee, clasp my left hand over my right wrist, and then draw my knee toward my chest. It is important to keep your left knee and right foot flat on the mat to get the most out of this stretch.

Cross Leg Stretch

This is another great stretching exercise for your hips, but it is a little more advanced. It is not something you should attempt in your first weeks or even months of training. It's a stretching exercise that you should strive for over the course of a year or two.

In the sitting position, I place my right foot on top of my left leg near the hip. Then I place my left foot on top of my right leg near the hip. If this position causes you pain, abandon this exercise until you acquire more flexibility.

With the cross-legged position no longer offering an adequate stretch, I lower my torso toward my feet and reach forward.

To take this stretch to its limit, I reach my hands all the way forward as I lower my torso and head down to the mat.

A Crazy Knee Stretch

Although this is somewhat unorthodox, I've found that this exercise gives my hamstrings, hips, and knees a good stretch. The goal is to be able to grab the foot of your extended leg, but it is important that you take this one slow.

From the sitting position, I straighten my right leg and place my left foot on top of my right knee. To keep my foot stationary, I grab the top of my left foot with my right hand. Keeping my right leg straight and flat on the mat, I place my left hand on my left knee and slowly apply downward pressure for the stretch.

Being flexible enough to place my left knee on the mat, I move onto the next phase of the stretch by pulling my left foot back to my right hip. Applying downward pressure on my left knee to keep it pinned to the mat, I lean slightly forward. It is important not to move onto the next step until you can hold this position comfortably.

With my left foot tucked into my right hip and my left knee pinned to the mat, I lean forward and grab the top of my right foot with both hands. This stretches my right hamstring, left knee, left hip, and my lower back. It is important to keep your right leg straight and pinned to the mat during the stretch. Hold this position for twenty or thirty seconds before switching sides.

Triangle Stretch

This is an excellent stretch for Rubber Guard players. Once you can get your foot somewhat close to your face, you will have little problem flowing into positions like Mission Control. Needless to say, it is also a great stretch for helping you develop a mean Triangle. The only real difference with this stretch and the submission is that your foot is in front of your knee rather than behind it.

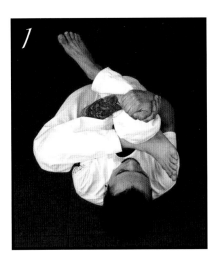

Lying flat on my back, I cross my left ankle over my right knee. Then I lift my right knee towards my chest, which draws my left foot closer to my face. To add pressure to the stretch, I reach my left hand underneath my left leg and over the top of my right knee. With my right palm facing toward me, I clasp my left hand around my right wrist just below my knee and slowly draw my legs toward my body. It is important to hold this stretch for twenty to thirty seconds before switching sides.

The Big Squeeze Stretch

This is similar to the previous exercise, except here I am reaching around both knees to get more of a stretch on my hips. Because this exercise requires flexible knees, you should stick with the original stretch until you can wrap both arms around your knees without causing pain.

Lying flat on my back, I cross my right leg over my left leg and then raise both knees toward my chest. Wrapping my arms around my legs, I clasp my hands together using a Gable Grip just below my knees. I then use my arm strength to slowly draw my knees into my torso. Hold for at least twenty seconds.

Double & Single Hip Stretch

Although the two hip stretches below can be found in almost every stretching book, I included them in this section because they should not be overlooked.

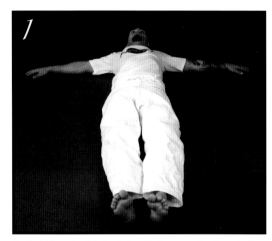

I start the stretch by lying flat on my back, splaying my arms out to my sides, and extending my legs. It is important to keep your palms on the mat and relax as much as possible.

After lifting both my knees up toward my chest, I slowly lower my legs to my left side. Notice how I keep my elbows and upper back locked to the mat. To get the most out of the stretch, I place my left hand on the top of my right knee and apply downward pressure.

Having held the double hip stretch for at least thirty seconds, I return to the starting position, bring my right knee up toward my chest, and then slowly lower it to my left side. Keeping my left leg, upper back, and elbows locked to the mat, I place my left hand on my right knee and apply downward pressure.

Downward Dog to Cobra

The downward dog to cobra does wonders to loosen up your abdomen and lower back, both of which can take some abuse while playing guard. The more flexible you are in these areas, the less chance you'll have of getting injured while rolling. It is important to note that if this exercise feels like a pushup, then you're doing it wrong. You should be as relaxed as possible as you make the transition between the two positions.

From the standing position, I lean forward and place both hands on the mat a shoulder's width apart. (It is important not to have your hands too close to your feet or too far apart.) Arching my back up into the air, I keep my eyes pointed at the mat and focus on breathing steadily and staying relaxed.

After taking a deep breath, I slowly start to exhale while dropping my groin down and forward. As my groin nears the mat, I rotate my hands outward for increased wrist mobility. I also lift my head toward the ceiling to get the most arc out of my back. Once you have held the position for twenty seconds, you can either end the stretch or transition back to the downward dog position.

Superman Stretch

Baseball pitchers warm up their throwing arm before heading out onto the field and sprinters stretch out their legs before bolting around the track. I don't do either of those sports; I train jiu-jitsu. That's why I do a plethora of exercises to warm up my lower back. A novice might not think that the lower back comes under that much pressure when rolling, but trust me when I tell you that it does. All the twisting and torquing adds up over the years. If you want to limit injuries down the road, you'll spend an ample amount of time before and after practice stretching your back muscles and forcing blood into the area. This is one of the better exercises you can do.

To begin the exercise, I get onto my hands and knees. Usually I'll spend a few seconds in this position to relax my body before beginning.

Lifting my right arm and left leg at the same time, I form a straight line from the tips of my fingers down to my toes. To maintain balance, I look in the direction my fingers are pointing. It is good to hold this position for twenty to thirty seconds before returning to the starting position. Usually I'll do this exercise three or four times before switching sides.

Lower Back Stretch

After taking a moment to relax and breathe in the starting position, you should do four or five repetitions with this exercise to loosen up your lower back.

Positioned on my hands and knees, I arch my back downward and take a massive breath.	As I steadily exhale, I tighten my stomach and attempt to pull my abdomen up through the small of my back. Once I have reached my full arch, I continue to contract my abdomen and push all air out of my lungs.	Once I have exhaled my entire breath, I slowly drop back down to the starting position. It is important to relax here for a couple seconds before taking your next breath and repeating the exercise.

Side/Back Stretch

Although this stretching exercise doesn't look like much, it can do wonders to loosen up and strengthen all the muscles around your hips, side, and lower back, which prepares you for all the twisting and turning you do while in the guard. I generally hold this position for about twenty to thirty seconds, come back down to the starting position, and then repeat four or five times.

Lying on my side, I prop my body up on my right elbow and right heel. To maintain balance, I grip my right wrist with my left hand and place my left foot on top of my right foot.	Basing off my right elbow and right heel, I lift my left hip toward the ceiling. Notice that my feet are heel to heel. This not only keeps me from getting off balance, but it also keeps my hips aligned with my body. Hold for at least twenty seconds.

Sit Up Back Stretch

As I have already mentioned, playing any type of guard can be brutal on your lower back. The stronger and more limber your back is, the less pain you will experience during and after practice. This exercise is key for both, as well as maximizing blood flow into your lower back to cut down on muscle pulls and tears.

Lying flat on my back, I raise my left knee. Here I am demonstrating how I will place my hands underneath my back. With both palms facing the mat, I place my right hand on top of my left. It is important to note that when you switch sides, you raise your right knee and place your left hand on top of your right.

Placing my hands palm down between the mat and my lower back, I take a deep breath.

Tightening my abdomen and exhaling slowly, I lift my head and shoulders off the mat. As I do this, I attempt to drive my lower back through my hands. When you exhale all your air, return to the starting position.

Chillin' Stretches

Whenever I'm chilling out, watching my students roll, or just watching TV, I'll grab one of my feet and torque on it to stretch out my knees, ankles, and hips. This not only helps me out while playing the Rubber Guard, but it also allows me to test my limitations. When I put myself in a heel hook, I realize just how far I can push it before I have to tap. Below are a few of the stretches that you might catch me doing during my alone time.

Chill Back Knee Stretch

Heel Hook Stretch

The Blunt Stretch

Part Two

HALF GUARD

Introduction to the Half Guard

In my opinion, the half guard is the most important position in jiu-jitsu because that is where the majority of battles are waged. A lot of jiu-jitsu practitioners would much rather obtain full guard, but it is a lot harder to trap an opponent between both of your legs. If you ignore the half guard, then you will be overlooking a major pathway to the top positions. You also won't develop total confidence when in the mount or side control because you're always worried about getting put onto your back, and this makes you less aggressive.

I realized the importance of the half guard early on in my training, and over the years I developed a system that turns the half guard into a highly offensive position where the mount, back, side control, and full guard are just a couple of movements away. My system revolves around a few basic steps and a host of sweeps that are based upon an opponent's reactions to your movements. No matter what your opponent does offensively or defensively, you're armed with an answer that will lead you to the top positions. Instead of being stuck when you obtain half guard, my system offers clear direction.

In order to gain this direction, the half guard should be viewed as a story that always has the same beginning. That beginning is the Lockdown, a simple positioning of your legs that is designed to frustrate your opponent with pain and make it very difficult for him to pass your half guard. In addition to boosting your confidence because it guarantees that your opponent won't be going anywhere in the immediate future, the Lockdown also distracts your opponent and bides you time to accomplish your next two tasks: Establishing the double under-hooks by utilizing The Jaws of Life and then whipping up to your side.

Once you get the Lockdown, secure the double under-hooks, and whip up to your side, the story changes every time. Usually I attempt Old School, a high percentage sweep that I devised early in my jiu-jitsu career. If my opponent sees Old School coming and posts his leg out, making the technique hard to execute, I transition into another sweep—the Twist Back, Plan B, the Electric Chair, or the Twist Back & Plan B Combo. As you will see in the upcoming section, your options are many. If my opponent is keen to my game and defending my sweeps, I can continue up to my knees into the Dogfight position where I have a handful of more options. If I have no luck sweeping my opponent from the Dogfight, I can execute a Limp Arm technique and transition into side control. To throw things up, I can even go directly from the whip up into the Dogfight. There are an infinite number of combinations that can be pieced together. Even if your opponent prevents you from getting the double under-hooks, I have included fail-safe options—The Stomp, The Super Stomp, The New Stomp—that allow you to transition to butterfly guard and remain offensive.

As long as you become a master at the half guard basics—securing the Lockdown, establishing the double under-hooks, and whipping up to your side—and then mix up the barrage of techniques you unleash upon your opponent, your overall game will improve significantly. Instead of trying to avoid the half guard, you will look to obtain the position because a clear route to the finish line is always within view. And the more comfortable you get with the half guard, the easier it will become to obtain. You will be surprised at how many opponents will simply fall into it. They accept the positioning because they are on top and already half passed your guard. They expect you to do what most jiu-jitsu practitioners do while in the half guard—spend all your time struggling to obtain full guard. They come ready to attack, and then suddenly they're doing little more than defending your Lockdown, double under-hooks, and your countless sweep attempts. As you flow from one technique to another, your opponent's confidence is shattered. After all, the man on top shouldn't be spending all his energy defending. As his will slowly drains away, more opportunities surface.

The ending to your half guard battle could be the mount, side control, or taking your opponent's back. It could be pulling full guard admits your opponent's confusion and then fully breaking him down, which allows you to start playing the Rubber Guard. It could be a submission anywhere along the way. Beginning the story the same and then never letting up allows you to write your own conclusion. As long as you have direction embedded in your mind, you will always have options at your disposal.

The trick is to work on your half guard as much as possible. After you have slapped the Lockdown on an opponent, he will probably look to defend it the next time he falls into your half guard. For this reason, you have to drill the Lockdown over and over. Learn how to fight for it. Learn how to slap it on an opponent who knows it's coming. Then learn how to battle for the double under-hooks and perfect the Whip Up. Before you know it, you will be able to do all three almost simultaneously.

The next step in your training should be to master the Old School sweep. Go for it again and again.

When your opponents get wise, test out the different options I have laid out in the upcoming pages and learn what works best for you. Bounce back and forth between half guard, full guard, and butterfly guard to discover the different pathways you can take. The half guard is a neutral position only for those who believe it to be.

Half Guard For MMA

With my system, the half guard isn't played that differently when you're training for Mixed Martial Arts competition. The main difference is that when you whip up to your side, you will use your bottom arm to guard against punches. This requires that you release one of your under-hooks, but that under-hook is easy to reestablish when you are ready to make a move.

The main difference with your alternate positioning is that you'll lessen the amount of blows you take while working for a sweep or submission. Will you still get punched? Probably. If you're looking for a half guard that will prevent you from getting punched, then you're going to be looking for a long time. Nothing is foolproof, and that is especially true when it comes to the guard. The trick is to utilize a system that will make it difficult for your opponent to hit you, as well as lessen the impact when he does. I find that the half guard system I've developed works pretty darn well. If you discover one that works better, send me a video, I wanna see!

The Lockdown

There are several different ways to trap an opponent in your half guard, but I have found the Lockdown to be by far the best one. I devised this technique early on in my jiu-jitsu training because every time I tried the most popular method, which is to trap your opponent's leg between your legs using a figure four, I got crushed. The reason I got crushed was because my opponent still had a solid base, making it easy for him to pass my guard into side control. Having a solid base also allowed my opponent to pin me to the mat, which hindered me from executing sweeps. It was more than a little frustrating because I was like most jiu-jitsu students new to the game in that I spent a considerable amount of time in my half guard. The reason I spent so much time there was because my full guard was always getting passed, leaving me with that single leg. Then I discovered the Lockdown. It allowed me to gain much better control over my opponent's trapped leg, and when I stretched the Lockdown out, it shattered his base. Suddenly my opponents weren't making these quick and easy transitions to side control. Suddenly they were having a much harder time pinning me to the mat, which allowed me to start experimenting with sweeps. I had no idea that the Lockdown was a judo technique—I came up with it out of sheer desperation, and it did wonders to improve my entire game.

Joe is in my half guard. In order to keep him from advancing to a more dominant position, I have to quickly secure the Lockdown.

Alternate Angle

I step my left foot over Joe's right leg. This hinders him from stepping his right leg over my right leg and moving into the side control position or sliding his right leg up between my legs and securing the mount position.

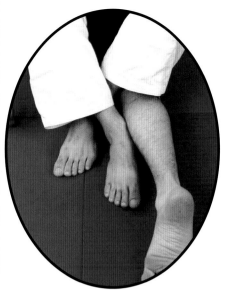

I step my right foot over my left, trapping Joe in my half guard.

I hook my right foot underneath Joe's right leg, securing the Lockdown position.

To stretch Joe out and destroy his base, I pinch my knees together and straighten out my legs. The more you straighten, the more pain you will inflict upon your opponent's calf muscle.

The Jaws of Life

Securing the Lockdown is a major component of playing an effective half guard, but the true challenge is to secure the double under-hooks. It's what allows you to turn what many people consider to be a stalemate position into a highly offensive one. Ideally, you want to secure an under-hook on the same side as the Lockdown before you break your opponent down into your guard, but this is sometimes hard to manage. In cases where this isn't possible, executing The Jaws of Life is a great option to acquire the under-hooks. It's important to execute this technique with speed. If your opponent sees The Jaws of Life coming, he'll most likely hold onto you even tighter and prevent you from creating space. But if you move decisively and with power, putting your opponent's neck in a good crank, it becomes very difficult for him to bring his head back down. If this technique fails and you just can't secure the double under-hooks, you can still transition to the butterfly guard using The Stomp, The New Stomp, or The Super Stomp, which you will learn about in the next section.

Joe is in my half guard with an over/under body lock. Although I have secured the Lockdown, I still need to establish an under-hook with my left arm.

To begin the battle for the double under-hooks, I place my left hand on Joe's right temple and then shove his head in the direction of two o'clock.

Having created some space between Joe's head and mine, I have enough room to place my right hand on top of my left. Now I use both arms to force Joe's head in the direction of two o'clock.

As I crank Joe's head in the direction of two o'clock, I create space between our bodies.

With my arms nearly extended, it becomes very difficult for Joe to muscle his head back down to my chest. This allows me to remove my right hand from his temple and slide it underneath his left arm. Notice how I wedge my right elbow between our bodies. This helps create space between us, which will allow me to wedge my left arm inside.

Creating a gap with my right arm, I slide my left elbow between Joe's torso and mine.

Gable Grip

There are many different ways to grip your hands together, but I prefer what I call the Gable Grip. To achieve this position, you want to clasp your hands together palm against palm without interlocking your thumbs. I feel this is the strongest grip one can use with the under-hooks, and it is also the least dangerous. When you interlock your thumbs, you run the risk of damaging them as your grip bends in different directions while rolling.

Pulling my arms out from between Joe's torso and mine, I loop my hands around his back and clasp my hands together using a Gable Grip, securing the double under-hooks.

The Whip Up

If you secure the double under-hooks but you're lying flat on your back, the double under-hooks really don't mean that much. To make the most out of the double under-hooks and turn the half guard into an offensive position, you first have to whip up onto your side. This technique is not easy to master. I know how difficult it can be when an opponent is driving an arm down into your neck, pinning you to the mat, but you must learn how to create space to execute the Whip Up. Just like every other technique, it must be drilled over and over. Have your training partner use all his might to hold you down, and then run through the move step by step until it feels completely natural. With many of the half guard techniques depending upon you being on your side, this move must come naturally before you attempt to learn the various sweeps.

Joe is in my half guard. I have secured the Lockdown and the double under-hooks, but Joe is driving his weight into me, pinning me flat on my back. Before I can get offensive, I first have to whip up to my side.

I momentarily release the double under-hooks and plant both hands on Joe's ribs.

In one explosive movement, I elevate Joe's leg using the Lockdown and push his body upward using my hands. It is important to notice that I'm not simply lifting Joe upward—I'm also using the Lockdown and my arms to rock his body toward my head. This pushes his base forward and creates enough space between us for me to whip up to my side.

As Joe rocks his weight back to reestablish his base, I follow him up and reach my left arm around his body, securing a left under-hook. I plant my right elbow on the mat, which helps me remain on my side.

Lying comfortably on my side, I lock my hands together using a Gable Grip. It is important to notice the positioning of my grip—it's digging into the soft spot between Joe's rib cage and hip.

Old School

In the beginning of my jiu-jitsu career, pretty much the only move I knew was the Twister. When I got an opponent's back, I nailed it a high percentage of the time. The problem was I had a hard time getting my opponent's back to pull it off. I spent a considerable amount of time working on setting up the Twister from the other positions, which paid off in the long run, but at the time it resulted in the other parts of my game being quite weak. I didn't have a strong guard, and my side control was nothing to write home about. Needless to say, opponents were passing my guard at will. My only defense was to pull them into my half guard. I had already discovered the Lockdown, but I didn't yet know what to do with it. I'd just squeeze my opponent's leg and hold on for dear life.

During one of these agonizing stalemates in the half guard, I started searching for something to grab onto, something to trap. Then I saw my opponent's foot sitting right there. I thought, "Hmmm, I wonder what would happen if I were to latch onto it?" It seemed to me that if I grabbed his far foot and pulled on it as hard as I could, I might be able to sweep him over. Just snatch it and run. So that is what I did, and it worked flawlessly. In the next couple of tournaments, the Old School Sweep was all that I did. I would just sit in half guard and wait for it. If there was a minute left on the clock, I would hold on for another thirty seconds, pull Old School to get on top, and then latch onto my opponent and try to stall my way to victory.

This was all back in '96. I was training with the Machados at the time, and they had never seen the Old School Sweep. They were virtually unstoppable in the competition circuit during the 80's, and I thought if they had never seen the move before, I must have made it up. They thought I had made it up. I didn't think I had invented the best move ever, but it worked pretty darn well. I continued to pull it off at tournaments all over Southern California. There were some pretty big players attending these tournaments, guys like Rickson Gracie, but I never thought any of them were watching me during my matches. Apparently some of them were.

Six years after Old School had first come to my rescue while in the half guard, I heard that Carlos Gracie Jr. was putting on a seminar at Rigan Machado's school in Torrance, California. Carlos was the son of the man who had invented Brazilian Jiu-Jitsu, the guy who brought the Machados under his wing and taught them. Knowing I had to check out this seminar, I threw my gi and brown belt in the trunk of my car and headed down there the day of the event. I ended up arriving a few minutes late and quickly got out onto the mat. While Carlos Jr. was doing his thing, showing everyone in attendance some kick ass moves, Jean Jacques and Rigan Machado came up to me and started asking about a new Twister set-up I had discovered off the sprawl. It absolutely blew my mind. Carlos Gracie Jr., one of the founders of Brazilian Jiu-Jitsu, was giving a seminar, and here the Machado brothers were inquiring about some Twister set-up I hardly every did. So I started showing them. Right in the middle of it, Fabio Vinelli came up and shushed the three of us. I couldn't believe it. The guy actually shushed the Machado brothers in their own academy. It was hilarious.

He directed our attention back to Carlos Gracie Jr., who was communicating with us through a translator. "This next move everyone now playing in half guard," the translator said in his broken English. "This new move everyone now playing in Brazil. Very popular new move."

The Machados and I looked at each other. We had completely forgotten about the Twister set-up. Immediately we were all wondering about this crazy new move everyone was doing down in Brazil. I was thinking that it had to be something sick, totally off the hook. So I'm sitting there watching, hanging off the edge of my seat, and all of a sudden Carlos Gracie Jr. shows Old School. The Machados glanced back at me, and the look they gave was, "What just happened there? That move isn't new. That is your move, Eddie."

Over the years I have taken a lot of flack over Old School. There are a lot of people claiming that Old School has been around for ages, that some guy named Gordo has been doing it since the dawn of time. I don't know this guy Gordo and I have never seen him pull off Old School, but I'm pretty sure he doesn't execute Old School using the Lockdown. I believe this because I had never seen a Brazilian Jiu-Jitsu player use the Lockdown before 2000. But that is neither here nor there. Truthfully, I don't really care if I made up Old School or not. It's a high percentage move that lands you in a favorable position. It was my bread and butter when I started out in jiu-jitsu, and it's still my bread and butter, especially when I'm rolling with guys who are familiar with my system. It's called Old School because that's exactly what it is.

Here I have already secured the Lock-down, established the double under-hooks, and whipped up to my side. I'm now in a position to set-up an attack on Joe.

Immediately noticing that Joe's foot is within reach, I use the momentum from the Whip Up to reach my right hand between his legs and latch onto his left foot. It's important to notice that I haven't let go of the Lock-down and that I'm gripping just above Joe's hip with my left under-hook.

Releasing the Lock-down, I turn more onto my right side. It is important that you keep your under-hook tight, as well as maintain a firm grasp on your opponent's foot.

Continuing to rotate my body, I come up to my knees and drive my weight forward into Joe. As I do this, I pull Joe's left foot out from underneath him with my right hand, destroying his base.

Still driving my weight into Joe, I step over his right leg and circle to my left to avoid being pulled into his half guard.

To assume the side control position, I drive my right knee into Joe's right hip and dig my left knee underneath his right shoulder. I then wrap my left arm underneath his head and my right arm underneath his left arm. Clasping my hands together underneath his left shoulder, I gain head and arm control. To keep Joe pinned to the mat, I drive my weight down into him.

Electric Chair Sweep / Submission

Once you've caught your training partner several times with Old School, expect him to start throwing some defense your way. He'll most likely post his leg out to prevent you from grabbing hold of his foot, making Old School hard to get. In such a scenario, the Electric Chair is an excellent alternative. In addition to being a high percentage sweep, it also gives you multiple options, all of which either land you in a top position or allow you to finish with a submission. It is important to drill these options because your window of opportunity to capitalize on them will come and go quickly. If you see an opening to apply the Electric Chair submission, go for it. If your opponent doesn't tap quickly, it probably means that he is too flexible to catch. You should then immediately continue with the sweep so you don't waste energy. I should also note that the Lockdown plays a key roll in this technique, so keep it tight. This is especially true with the various options that stem off the initial sweep.

I secured the Lockdown, fought for the double under-hooks, and then whipped up onto my side. I'm now in a perfect position to set up an attack on Joe.

Joe senses the Old School Sweep coming and posts his left leg out to prevent me from grabbing his foot.

Realizing I can't execute Old School, I decide to go for the Electric Chair. Without hesitating, I reach my right hand around the back of Joe's posted leg and hook my wrist around his thigh.

4

Whipping my legs upward, I pull Joe's right leg off the mat with the Lockdown to redistribute the majority of his weight from his legs to his arms. This allows me to bring my left arm underneath his body and hook my wrist over his left armpit. I then push off with my left hand, which helps me rotate my body in a counterclockwise direction and sink my right hand deeper around his left leg.

5

Continuing to rotate in a counterclockwise direction using my hooks, I reach my right arm all the way around Joe's left leg. This traps his right leg between my head and right shoulder. At the same time, I push on Joe's left triceps with my left hand, forcing him forward and collapsing his base.

6

Clasping my hands together using a Gable Grip, I stretch Joe out in the Lockdown and drive my right shoulder toward the mat. This puts a tremendous amount of pressure on Joe's groin, but because he is super flexible, he doesn't tap to the ELECTRIC CHAIR SUBMISSION. Instead of holding on and wasting energy, I decide to abandon the submission and transition back into the sweep.

7

I release my Gable Grip and post my left arm on the mat. Still extending the Lockdown, I use my right arm to keep Joe's right leg tight against my neck as I drive my body toward him.

8

As I come up onto my knees on top of Joe, I drive my right shoulder toward the mat and start my pass into side control.

MASTERING THE RUBBER GUARD

Still driving my right shoulder toward the mat, I slide my left arm beneath Joe's head and clasp my hands together using a Gable Grip.

Releasing the Lockdown, I step my right leg out from between Joe's legs.

I bring my left knee up and wedge it underneath Joe's right shoulder.

I let go of Joe's right leg and establish side control.

Stoner Control

The first thing I will do when performing the Electric Chair Sweep is test the submission. If the submission doesn't work because my opponent is too flexible, I'll sit up and complete the sweep. However, sometimes I can't sit up because my opponent is too tall or he is basing out on his hands. Instead of fighting him and wasting energy, I abandon my former path and transition to a position I call Stoner Control, which opens up a lot of options. This particular technique will land you in side control just like the previous Electric Chair Sweep—it's just a different way to get there based upon your opponent's reactions.

I've got to this position by utilizing the Electric Chair Sweep. Here I'm extending the Lockdown, keeping my right arm tight around Joe's left leg, and pushing on his left arm with my left hand to steal his base. I'm trying to catch Joe in the Electric Chair submission, but he is too flexible. My best option would be to continue with the Electric Chair Sweep, but Joe is still posting on his arms, making the sweep hard to execute. As a result, I decide to transition to Stoner Control.

Reaching my left hand behind my head, I grab the back of Joe's left ankle and start maneuvering his foot to the front of my face. Notice how I am still stretching Joe out with the Lockdown. If you release that pressure, it will give your opponent an opportunity to escape.

As I bring Joe's left foot in front of my face, I slide my right hand up to his ankle to help move his foot to the left side of my head. My goal is to clear his leg so I can sit up, and two hands accomplish the job better than one.

Having brought Joe's leg around to the left side of my head, I quickly sit up and wrap both arms around his waist, achieving the Stoner Control position. It is important to hug your opponent's waist really tight, as well as keep your armpit pressed tightly against his back. Your opponent's main goal will be to free his trapped leg, and you need to prevent him from achieving his goal by eliminating all space.

As I come up to my knees, Joe rolls over onto his right shoulder and tries to turn away from me in an effort to free his leg. I follow his path, staying nice and tight to shut his efforts down. As long as I keep his left leg trapped, he won't be able to pull me into his guard.

Releasing the Lockdown, I back step my left leg in a counter-clockwise direction to clear Joe's legs and prevent him from pulling me into his guard.

Once my left leg had cleared Joe's legs, I plant my right knee underneath his left shoulder and my left knee underneath his hip. Sliding my right arm underneath Joe's head, I clasp my hands together using a Gable Grip and secure side control.

Stoner Control Variation

Stoner Control can cause quite a bit of discomfort for your opponent. With his legs all tangled up, there is a good chance he will try to get on top by twisting his body into you and wrapping an arm around your head. If you use this technique to roll with him, you will end up in side control. Just as with the previous Electric Chair technique from Stoner Control, it is important to maintain a tight Lockdown and stay snug to your opponent.

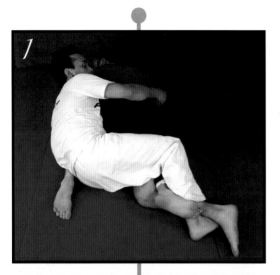

I couldn't get the Electric Chair finish, so I moved into Stoner Control by bringing Joe's leg over my head, sitting up, and wrapping my arms tightly around his hips. Notice that I have his left leg trapped.

Instead of turning away from me as he did in the previous technique, Joe turns into me and wraps his left arm around my head in an effort to get on top.

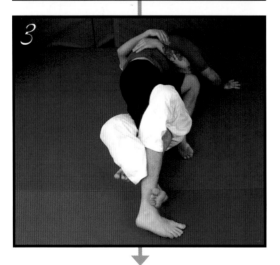

Because Joe's left arm is wrapped around my head, he can no longer post his left hand on the mat, which allows me to roll him to my right. As I execute the roll, I ensure Joe comes with me by hugging his waist tight and keeping the Lockdown secure.

Having rolled Joe all the way over to his back, my next goal is to untangle my legs and transition into side control.

Releasing the Lockdown, I slide my right leg out from underneath Joe's left leg. Next I unhook my left leg and pull it free of Joe's legs.

With head and arm control, I dig my knees into Joe's left side and establish the side control position.

Stoner Control Arm Triangle

This technique is based upon the same scenario as the last. You have your opponent in Stoner Control and he attempts to untangle his legs by turning into you. Instead of rolling him over to his back and transitioning into side control as you did in the previous move, here you are going to catch him in an Arm Triangle.

I couldn't get the Electric Chair finish, so I moved into Stoner Control by bringing Joe's leg over my head, sitting up, and wrapping my arms tightly around his hips. Notice that I have his left leg trapped.	As Joe turns into me, he tries to wrap his left arm around my head in an effort to get on top. To stop him from doing this, I climb my body upward and trap his left arm against the left side of my head. I then reach my left arm around the back of his head.	Bringing my right arm up, I cup my left hand around my right biceps. I then place my right hand on the right side of my face, locking everything tight. To apply the Triangle choke, I drive my head down into Joe's arm and squeeze my arms together. It is important to notice that I haven't let go of the Lockdown.

Stoner Control Calf Crank

This is another good option off Stoner Control when an opponent turns into you. It requires letting go of his hips, which means you have to be quick. You want to lock in the submission before your opponent realizes that he has a chance to escape by pulling his trapped leg free.

Unable to get the Electric Chair Submission, I moved into Stoner Control by bringing Joe's leg over my head, sitting up, and wrapping my arms tightly around his hips. Notice that I have his left leg trapped.	Keeping the Lockdown intact, I lift Joe's right leg with my right foot. This allows me to grab his foot with my right hand.	Reaching my left arm around to the backside of Joe's body, I latch onto the top of his foot with my left hand. To apply the Calf Crank submission, I pull Joe's right foot into my body using both hands.

Twist Back & Plan B Combo

This is another one of my favorite sweeps to execute when my opponent posts his leg out to prevent me from getting Old School. I stumbled upon it not long ago while I was playing around with the Twist Back, a half guard sweep where I carry my opponent over using the double under-hooks. On this particular day I couldn't get my opponent over with the double under-hooks, so I cupped one hand around his outside leg—a grip I use in another half guard sweep called Plan B. So basically I was trying to combine two moves into one to see what happened, and the result was awesome. Both of the original sweeps are still worthy of being learned and drilled, but this one stands on a whole different level. Coming up with it reminded me just how important it is to constantly experiment. Once you learn all the basics of my system and have drilled every sweep over and over, you should play around with the different moves as much as possible during practice. If you are like most of my students, you'll start coming up with moves of your own that better fit your body, style, and personality.

After securing the Lockdown, I battled for the double under-hooks and whipped up to my side. I'm now in a perfect position to launch an attack on Joe.

Releasing the Lockdown, I hook Joe's right leg with my left ankle and then curl my leg back toward my buttocks. This puts a tremendous amount of pressure on Joe's right knee, which will help me roll him over my body and to my left.

Releasing my Gable Grip, I C-cup the inside of Joe's posted left leg with my right hand. At the same time, I bring my left foot down to the mat. It is important to notice how my left leg is bent over Joe's right calf, keeping it locked tight.

Using my left hand to pull down on Joe's left hip, I force my coiled left knee to the mat. At the same time, I push off the mat with my right foot and drive Joe's left leg upward with my right hand. My combined efforts sends Joe over-top of me and down toward his back.

I follow Joe over and turn into him. It is important to note that Joe is doing everything he can to turn back into me in the hopes of transitioning into the half guard or butterfly guard. I'm stopping him from achieving this by maintaining downward pressure on his left leg with my right hand and keep-ing my left leg curled tight around his right calf.

Continuing to turn into Joe, I pull my left leg out from underneath his right leg. I then dig my knees under his right side to establish side control with an over/under body lock.

Half Guard to Closed Guard

When Old School fails, you have a lot of options—Plan B, the Twist Back, the Twist Back & Plan B Combo, the Electric Chair. Throw as many of these techniques at your opponent as possible. Even if he manages to shut them all down, you will still have stolen his attention. While he is anticipating another sweep, you can make an easy transition to full guard. And the nice thing about this technique is that it lands you in full guard with your opponent already broken down, which is a major plus. From there, you can instantly start playing the Rubber Guard.

After securing the Lockdown, I battled for the double under-hooks and whipped up to my side. I'm now in a perfect position to launch an attack on Einstein.

I reach for Einstein's foot to execute Old School, but he sees it coming and posts his leg out.

Releasing the Lockdown, I post my right hand on Einstein's left leg to keep it at bay. This allows me to bring my right knee up.

Still keeping Einstein's leg at bay, I bring my right knee towards my chest so I can slip my right foot over his left leg.

Once I clear my right foot over Einstein's leg, I achieve closed guard by hooking my feet together behind his back. From here I will instantly start playing the Rubber Guard by trapping one of Einstein's hands to the mat and transitioning into New York, which you will learn about in the Rubber Guard section.

Transition to the Dogfight

As you become proficient with my system, the Whip Up will get easier and easier. Before you know it, you will be able to whip up to your elbow. Once you can accomplish this, there is nothing stopping you from whipping all the way up to your knees to challenge your opponent in the Dogfight position. It is a wonderful position to wage battle, but your intentions heading in shouldn't be set in stone. The reason for this is simple—when entering the Dogfight from the bottom position, you will have an under-hook and your opponent will have a Whizzer. The Whizzer is a little more powerful because your opponent can put his weight behind it. If your opponent is a weak wrestler, you might be able to overcome the power of his Whizzer with your under-hook, allowing you to catch him with the Half and Half sweep or Plan B. If your opponent is a strong wrestler with a powerful Whizzer, this probably won't be possible. Instead of trying to battle your opponent with your under-hook, you should counter his powerful Whizzer with a Limp Arm technique, which you will learn about shortly. If you don't have a good feeling for your opponent's wrestling prowess heading into the Dogfight, testing the Half and Half will quickly inform you. The important thing to remember about the Dogfight is that it has earned its name justly. Expect a mean, dirty battle. No single path will work with every opponent, so learning all your possibilities is a must.

After securing the Lockdown, I battled for the double under-hooks and whipped up onto my right elbow. Instead of going for Old School, I have decided to transition to the Dogfight.

Releasing the Lockdown, I drive my under-hook into Joe and come up onto my knees. Notice how I post my right arm further out as I turn into Joe.

As I come all the way up to my knees, I keep my body pressed tightly against Joe's body and maintain a deep under-hook. Notice how I have hooked my left leg under Joe's right instep and sat back. This prevents him from escaping. It also prevents him from obtaining butterfly guard or full guard if he should turn into me. It's important to remember to do this because it keeps you from having to fight for positioning in an unnecessary scramble.

Half and Half

The Half and Half sweep is a technique I started using early on in my jiu-jitsu career when I discovered the power of the under-hooks in the half guard. It works great off the Whip Up, and it works a high percentage of the time against opponents who don't have an unusually strong Whizzer. Sometimes I'll just whip up into the Dogfight position, and if my opponent doesn't have a good Whizzer at the ready, I'll use that upward momentum and tackle him over. It can be as simple as squeezing your under-hooks really tight into the soft tissue of your opponent's side and then driving your head into him. However, when rolling with a good wrestler or someone who understands my system, you'll probably encounter some serious resistance. In such cases, you have a better chance of obtaining a more dominant position by utilizing the Half and Half Variation or a Limp Arm technique.

I'm up on my knees, battling Joe's over-hook with my under-hook in the Dogfight position.

Joe doesn't have a strong Whizzer locked in, so I decide to execute the Half and Half. Reaching my right arm underneath Joe's body, I clasp my hands together using a Gable Grip and dig my grip into the soft portion of his left side (just below his rib cage and just above his hip). Squeezing my arms as tightly as possible, I drive my head into Joe and topple his base.

Continuing to squeeze with my body lock, I push the entire weight of my body into Joe and force him over onto his side. Notice how I still have my left leg hooked around Joe's right calf to prevent him from pulling guard.

Keeping my left leg hooked underneath Joe's right calf, I step my right foot in a clockwise direction.

Once my right leg is clear of Joe's legs, I pull my left leg out from underneath his calf and transition into the side control position.

Half and Half Variation

While I was training Chuck Liddell for his second fight against Randy Couture in the Ultimate Fighting Championships, I was showing him the regular Half and Half and he came up with this variation. I quickly found that it works wonderfully when you're executing the standard Half and Half, your opponent is almost over, and then you suddenly encounter resistance. Although your opponent is battling back by pushing into you, all you have to do to collapse his base is reach underneath his body, hook his knee, and pull it toward you. With your opponent's base collapsed, you can really drive your under-hook and head into him, making for an easy transition into side control.

I've worked up to my knees to battle Joe in the Dogfight position. Notice how I have hooked my left leg under Joe's right instep and sat back. This prevents him from escaping. It also prevents him from obtaining butterfly guard or full guard if he should turn into me. It's important to remember to do this because it keeps you from having to fight for positioning in an unnecessary scramble.

Posting on my right leg, I drive into Joe with my left under-hook and head.

Still driving into Joe, I reach my right hand underneath his body and grip the outside of his left knee.

Continuing to drive my weight into Joe, I use my right hand to pull his left knee out from underneath him and collapse his base. It is important to notice how tight I am to Joe. If you don't maintain this pressure, your opponent will be able to use his Whizzer to overpower your sweep and get back to his knees.

Still driving my weight down into Joe and gripping his left knee with my right hand, I back step my right leg over my left and plant it on the mat.

Once my right leg is clear, I slide my left leg out from underneath Joe's right leg and transition into side control with an over/under body lock.

Plan B

When I get to the Dogfight position, I'll usually test out the Half and Half to see if I can blast through my opponent and make a quick transition to side control. It would be nice if this worked every time, but that just isn't the case. Thankfully I have backup techniques. If my opponent has an incredible strong Whizzer that completely overpowers my under-hook, then I will utilize a Limp Arm technique. However, if the resistance I encounter has to do with a strong base rather than a strong Whizzer, then I will usually resort to Plan B. It works great immediately after the Half and Half because you're sweeping your opponent in the opposite direction, which can catch him off guard.

I've worked up to my knees to battle Joe in the Dogfight position. Notice how I have hooked my left leg under Joe's right instep and sat back. This prevents him from escaping. It also prevents him from obtaining butterfly guard or full guard if he should turn into me. It's important to remember to do this because it keeps you from having to fight for positioning in an unnecessary scramble.

As I drive my weight into Joe, he resists and pushes back with his Whizzer. Instead of trying to fight his over-hook with my under-hook, I decide to resort to Plan B and sweep him in the opposite direction. I start the sweep by reaching my right hand underneath his body and establishing a C-cup grip behind his left knee.

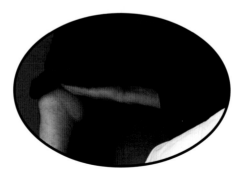

Dropping to my right shoulder, Joe's weight falls into me. With his base disrupted, I quickly roll him over the top of my body by pulling on his left hip with my left hand, pushing up on his left leg with my right hand, and forcing his right foot towards my buttocks by curling my left leg. It is important to note that the harder your opponent drives into you while in the Dogfight position, the easier this roll will be.

As I continue to roll Joe over my body by pushing on his left leg with my right hand and pulling on his left hip with my left hand, I keep both legs curled tight to stop him from freeing his right leg.

Completing the roll, I drive my right knee into Joe's hip and continue to push on his left leg with my right hand. These two actions prevent him from scrambling and pulling me into his guard.

Bringing my left knee up to Joe's side, I establish an over/under body lock and obtain the side control position.

Twist Back & Plan B Combo

The Twist Back & Plan B Combo is another technique I'll use in the Dogfight when my opponent's base is really strong and I can't get the Half and Half. The regular Plan B also works, but this one has a better success rate.

I've worked up to my knees to battle Joe in the Dogfight position. Notice how I have hooked my left leg under Joe's right instep and sat back. This prevents him from escaping. It also prevents him from obtaining butterfly guard or full guard if he should turn into me. It's important to remember to do this because it keeps you from having to fight for positioning in an unnecessary scramble.

Although it is hard to see in these pictures, I hook my right foot around the back of Joe's right knee.

I reach my right hand underneath Joe's body and C-cup the inside of his right leg.

As I roll over onto my right shoulder, I squeeze my left leg into my buttocks while pushing my right foot out. This twists Joe's knee in the direction of the roll. At the same time, I also pull Joe's body over with my left hook and drive his leg up with my right hand.

As Joe rolls over onto his shoulders, I continue to drive his right leg upward with my right foot and push on his left leg with my right hand.

Joe rolls all the way over to his back and I follow him over. As I sit up to establish side control, I continue to push on his left leg with my right hand. This keeps him from turning back into me and pulling guard.

Sitting all the way up, I move into the side control position and establish an over/under body lock.

The Powder Keg

Throwing non-stop sweep attempts at your opponent while in the Dogfight position is a great way to distract him. Once he is using all his weight and might and concentration to block the Half and Half and Plan B options, there is a good chance he won't see the Triangle coming.

I'm up on my knees, battling Joe in the Dogfight position. Instead of wrapping my under-hook around Joe's body and latching onto his side, I loop it around his head and grab hold of his trap muscle. This sets me up for the Triangle.

Posting my weight on my right arm, I throw my right leg underneath Joe. As I do this, I use my left grip to maintain balance.

Turning my body in a counterclockwise direction, I come down onto my right elbow and whip my right leg around the left side of Joe's head.

As I finish my counterclockwise rotation and come down onto my back, I release my left grip on Joe's trap and wrap my right leg around the back of his head. To secure my right leg in place and lock in the Triangle, I bring my left leg up and hook it over my right foot.

Straightening my leg across the back of Joe's neck, I clasp my hands together behind his head using a Gable Grip. To apply the Triangle choke, I pinch my knees together and pull his head down toward my chest with both arms.

DPO to Side Control

The Limp Arm is an old wrestling move that works beautifully in my half guard game. It comes in particularly handy in the Dogfight position when your opponent has a really powerful Whizzer. As your opponent drives you down with his over-hook, you simply release your under-hook and let your arm go limp. When done quickly, there is a good chance that you'll catch your opponent by surprise, causing him to get overextended and fall forward to his side. Then it becomes very easy to sweep him over and obtain side control. The key to success with this move is to control your opponent by sitting on his foot and really making him commit to his Whizzer. The more he commits, the more overextended he will become when you let your arm go limp. It's a great way to switch things up against a powerful wrestler when Old School and Half and Half don't work.

You might be wondering why I named this technique DPO rather than Limp Arm, and the answer is simple. The move is so popular among wrestlers, the second your teammates call the technique out to you in competition, your opponent will know exactly what you are planning to do and prepare to defend the Limp Arm. Changing the name is just a way to hide your intentions. When trying to decide on a name, the guys in my gym thought of everything that would make a guy go limp, and there were two favorites. The first was "Jason's dick," referring to the dick of Jason Chambers, my top MMA student. We all concluded that such a sight would most certainly make us go limp. The other was "dead pussy order." We were about half and half, so we decided to vote on it. Everything was very democratic. After tallying all the votes, Dead Pussy Order (DPO) won by a narrow victory.

I've worked up to my knees to battle Joe in the Dogfight position. Notice how I have hooked my left leg under Joe's right instep and sat back. This is really important when doing the Limp Arm because once you free your arm, there's going to be a small window of opportunity for your opponent to escape before you can establish side control or take his back. As long as you keep that leg trapped, you have nothing to worry about.

Joe is driving his weight into me with a really strong Whizzer. Instead of fighting him, I give in to it by falling forward. As I do this, I let my arm go completely limp.

Because I have let my arm go limp, it slips free of Joe's over-hook.

Once my arm is free, Joe's balance is thrust forward. I capitalize by quickly coming up, wrapping my left arm around his back, and driving my weight into him.

Continuing to drive my weight into Joe, he collapses onto his back. I back step with my right leg and begin to move into side control.

Securing an over/under body lock, I dig my knees into Joe's right side and obtain side control.

DPO to Back

A lot of times when you let your arm go limp in the Dogfight, your opponent will fall to his side, making for an easy transition to side control. But other times your opponent will face plant into the mat and then try to recover. If such a scenario should occur, you want to immediately take his back. This must be drilled over and over because if you're slow making the transition, your opponent will have a chance to recover and back out, take you down, or stand up. It is also important to note that when taking your opponent's back you will need to establish an over/under body lock to maintain the position.

I've worked up to my knees to battle Joe in the Dogfight position. Notice how I have hooked my left leg under Joe's right instep and sat back. This is really important when doing the Limp Arm because once you free your arm, there's going to be a small window of opportunity for your opponent to escape before you can establish side control or take his back.

Joe is driving his weight into me with a really strong Whizzer.

Instead of fighting Joe's Whizzer, I give into it by falling forward and letting my arm go completely limp.

Letting my arm go limp has forced Joe to over commit and fall forward.

With Joe's base and balance disrupted, I quickly wrap my left arm around his back.

Instead of falling down to his left side as I drive into him, Joe falls face down to the mat. Instantly I recognize that his weight is distributed primarily to his right side, making the standard DPO hard to execute. Adapting to the situation, I wrap my right arm around Joe's neck and clasp my hands together using a Gable Grip. This gives me an over/under body lock, which allows me to work to take his back.

Drowning Wizard

This is another option when going up against an opponent with a powerful Whizzer in the Dogfight position. It can be a difficult move to pull off in the beginning, but it's a good option because instead of transitioning into side control or taking your opponent's back, you're setting him up for a submission. It's executed the same as the previous Limp Arm technique, except instead of letting your arm go entirely limp, you want to let it go half limp so you can hook your opponent's arm. It takes some practice to master, but once you get it down, the Spider Web position and all its submissions are just a few steps away.

I've worked up to my knees to battle Joe in the Dogfight position. Notice how I have hooked my left leg under Joe's right instep and sat back. This is really important when doing the Limp Arm because once you free your arm, there will be a small window of opportunity for your opponent to escape before you can establish side control or take his back.

Posting my weight on my right hand, I slide my right leg underneath Joe's body.

Rotating my body in a clockwise direction, I let my left arm go partially limp. You don't want to let your arm go completely limp with this technique because your intentions are not to free your arm. Your goal is to capture your opponent's arm by getting the crook of your elbow hooked around the crook of your opponent's elbow. If you don't achieve that, your opponent will be able to pull his arm free and escape your submission attempt.

Keeping my left arm hooked tight around Joe's right arm, I bring my left leg over his back as I continue to turn my body in a clockwise direction.

Bringing my left leg all the way over Joe's back, I slide my shin across the right side of his face as I drive my knee down toward the mat.

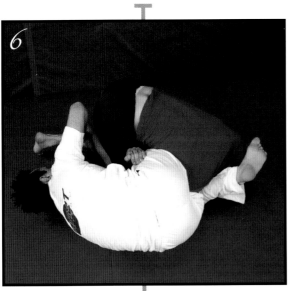

As I start to roll over onto my left shoulder, Joe is forced into a forward roll. I assist his roll by grabbing his right leg with my left hand and forcing it upward. It is important to notice that I'm reaching my left hand across my body and latching onto my right hip. This allows me to maintain a really tight hook on Joe's trapped arm, making it very difficult for him to pull his arm free.

As I continue with my roll, I help Joe's body over by guiding his right leg with my right hand. I'm still gripping my right hip with my left hand to keep Joe's right arm trapped to my body.

As Joe rolls over onto his back, I do two things simultaneously. I place my left leg over the top of his head, which sets me up to attack his arm, and I reach my right arm under his right leg to prevent a scramble. This puts me in the Spider Web position, from which I have numerous submission options. To learn about these options, see the Spider Web section.

The Stomp

By now you probably understand the foundation of my half guard game—establish the Lockdown, secure the double under-hooks, and then whip up to your side into the attack position. It's a highly aggressive system when you can achieve all three goals, but sometimes you encounter blockades along the way. One of those major blockades can be getting the double under-hooks. If your opponent has freaky strong head and arm control, it might not be possible to execute The Jaws of Life and get your second under-hook. You're going to be gridlocked with one over-hook and one under-hook. A good option in such a scenario is to transition to butterfly guard with your over-hook using The Stomp. Once in butterfly guard, your opponent will be forced to release his head and arm control because you can sweep him over if he doesn't. This allows you to sit up in the butterfly guard and obtain a position I call The Cocoon.

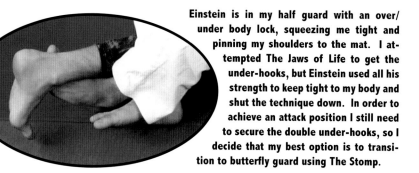

Einstein is in my half guard with an over/under body lock, squeezing me tight and pinning my shoulders to the mat. I attempted The Jaws of Life to get the under-hooks, but Einstein used all his strength to keep tight to my body and shut the technique down. In order to achieve an attack position I still need to secure the double under-hooks, so I decide that my best option is to transition to butterfly guard using The Stomp.

I wrap my right arm around Einstein's left arm to secure a tight over-hook. At the same time, I push off Einstein's right hip with my left hand, driving his hips back toward my legs.

I release the Lockdown by bringing my left foot out from underneath Einstein's left leg. Without wasting time, I immediately stomp my left foot down on his calf, curling my toes to hinder him from freeing his leg. This pins his left leg to the mat. As I do this, I continue to push on his right hip with my left hand to force his base back toward my legs.

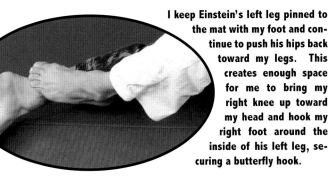

I keep Einstein's left leg pinned to the mat with my foot and continue to push his hips back toward my legs. This creates enough space for me to bring my right knee up toward my head and hook my right foot around the inside of his left leg, securing a butterfly hook.

Continuing to push on Einstein's right hip with my left hand, I use my butterfly hook to spread his left leg away from his right. Having created the needed separation, I release The Stomp and pull my left leg up between his legs.

After hooking my left foot around the inside of Einstein's right leg, he sits back to reestablish his base. Following him up, I keep my right arm hooked tightly over his left arm and reach my left arm underneath his right arm for an under-hook. This puts me in the Cocoon. From here I have a number of options, including transitioning back to half guard with the under-hook to attempt a sweep. To learn more about your options from the Cocoon, visit the butterfly section.

The Super Stomp

The original stomp is the best technique to utilize for going from half guard to butterfly guard because it offers the most control. However, sometimes it can be difficult to establish your second butterfly hook. The Super Stomp comes in handy in such a scenario.

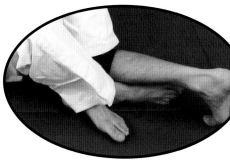

Einstein is in my half guard, pinning my shoulders to the mat with an over/under body lock. I have already attempted The Jaws of Life, but he shut the technique down by clinging to me with all his might.

After hooking my left arm over Einstein's right arm, I drive his hips down towards my legs with my right hand

Continuing to drive Einstein's hips down with my right hand, I release the Lockdown, slide my right foot out from underneath his right leg, and then stomp on the bottom of his right calf to pin his leg to the mat. It is important to notice that the toes of my right foot are curled in to better trap Einstein's leg.

I maneuver my left leg around to the inside of Einstein's right thigh, which gives me a left butterfly hook. I then lift Einstein's right leg with my butterfly hook, as well as swing my right leg upward. This elevates Einstein's right hip, which gives me enough room to slide my right leg up between his legs and establish my second butterfly hook.

Taking advantage of the space I created, I pull my right leg up and hook my right foot around the inside of Einstein's left leg.

As Einstein sits back to keep from getting swept, I sit up with him. Keeping my left over-hook tight, I reach my right arm underneath his left arm to establish an under-hook. This puts me in the Cocoon position.

The New Stomp

The New Stomp is just one big blast. It's straight up 10th Planet Kung Fu. It varies from the previous move because instead of stomping the back of your opponent's ankle, you're going to hook under that ankle and lift it up, creating the space needed to get your butterfly hook. It's a sight to behold when your successful with it, but it's a mess when you aren't. You risk losing control of your opponent's leg, which gives him an opportunity to pass. For such reasons, it is not as effective or safe as the original Stomp, which controls the heck out of your opponent.

Einstein is in my half guard, pinning my shoulders to the mat with an over/under body lock. I have already attempted The Jaws of Life, but his hold was too strong.

After hooking my right arm over Einstein's left arm, I push his hips down towards my legs with my left hand.

Although I release the Lockdown, I keep my left foot hooked underneath Einstein's left foot. As I lift my left leg, it pulls Einstein's left leg off the mat. Continuing to drive his hips back with my left hand, I coil my right leg up to establish my first butterfly hook.

I continue to push off Einstein's right hip with my left hand and lift his left leg with my left hook. These two actions give me enough room to coil my right foot around his left hip and establish my first butterfly hook.

Driving Einstein's left leg upward with my right butterfly hook creates enough space for me to quickly slide my left knee between his legs and establish my second butterfly hook. Now that I am in the butterfly guard position, Einstein will most likely sit back to avoid being swept.

Before I can sweep Einstein, he sits back. As he does this, I sit up with him, using my right over-hook to keep him tight to my upper body.

As I sit all the way up, I keep my right over-hook tight and reach my left arm underneath Einstein's right arm to establish an under-hook. This lands me in the Cocoon position, which gives me many options. To learn those options, see the butterfly section.

The Godfather

Just like The Stomp, The Godfather is another technique you can use in the half guard when you can't get the double under-hooks. Instead of putting you in the butterfly guard, the technique will land you in full guard. Sometimes you will get lucky and be able to sweep your opponent all the way over to his back, but most of the time he'll shut the sweep down by posting and spinning back into you. As long as you keep your leg high, you'll be able to trap him in your full guard when he comes. I've frustrated more than a few opponents with technique, and every time I feel like whispering a quote from The Godfather III—"Just when you thought you were out, you get pulled back in." And in addition to frustrating your opponent, The Godfather will also put you into full guard with an over-hook, which is key. Because your opponent's hand is already on the mat, you don't have to break him down. It allows you to really go to work. You can clear your opponent's neck and get to Chill Dog or you can go to the Pyramid—two dead zones you will learn about in the Rubber Guard section.

Einstein is in my half guard, pinning my shoulders to the mat with an over/under body lock. I have already attempted The Jaws of Life, but his hold was too strong.

I hook my left arm over Einstein's right arm.

Keeping my left over-hook tight, I slide my left leg out to my left side. Notice how I am curling my leg. This twists Einstein's right leg and draws his weight over to my left side. At the same time, I push on Einstein's left hip with my right hand, which also helps move his weight toward my left.

As I push off my right leg and turn onto my left side, I drop my left knee to the mat. Note how I keep my left leg curled tight to prevent Einstein from freeing his trapped right leg. You should also note how I have kept my left over-hook nice and tight. This is important because if your over-hook is loose, your opponent will be able to pull his arm free and use it to post.

Einstein stops the sweep by posting with his right leg, which is exactly what I expected. Notice how he doesn't have anywhere to go except back into me.

Pushing off his right leg, Einstein swings back into me. As he does this, I lift my right knee so I can catch him in my closed guard. Notice how my over-hook is still tight, and that I'm still trapping Einstein's right leg by keeping my left leg curled. If I were to let up on either, Einstein could easily slip out. Then he could move back into my half guard or even obtain side control.

As Einstein turns into me, I throw my right leg over his back. To capture him in my full guard, I bring my left leg around his back and hook my feet together. Notice how Einstein is broken down into my guard and that I've trapped his right hand to the mat with my over-hook. From here I can instantly start playing the Rubber Guard.

Godfather Sweep to Side Control

If you execute The Godfather with speed and power, sometimes you can get the sweep before your opponent has a chance to post his leg. In such a scenario, you can simply follow him over and obtain side control.

Einstein is in my half guard, pinning my shoulders to the mat with an over/under body lock. I have already attempted The Jaws of Life, but his hold was too strong.

I unhook my feet and straighten out my left leg, hooking Einstein's right foot in the process.

I curl my left leg in toward my buttocks. Notice how Einstein's right leg gets bent at an odd angle. This disrupts his base and will help me sweep him over.

I sweep Einstein over to his back by driving off my right foot and pushing up on his left hip with my right hand. Notice how I am still torquing his leg by keeping my left leg curled tight.

Einstein doesn't manage to post his left leg, which allows me to sweep him all the way over to his back. As he lands, I immediately come up on top of him. Notice how I still have my left leg curled tightly over his right leg.

Once I have my weight distributed on top of Einstein, I release my hook on his leg and pull my left leg underneath my right leg. Immediately I bring my left knee up to his right shoulder.

To secure side control, I bring my right knee up to Einstein's left hip and establish an over/under body lock.

The Stakeout

If your opponent knows that you're trying to pull guard, it's a lot easier to trap him in your half guard than it is to get him in your full guard. No halfway decent jiu-jitsu practitioner will simply let you pull full guard. You could try a couple of tricks to see if you can do it, but those tricks generally have a low success rate. Half guard is much easier because most opponents won't put up such a fight to avoid it. In addition to putting them on top, they are already half passed your guard. However, once you get good at my system and have caught your training partners in numerous half guard sweeps, you might encounter some resistance when going for the Lockdown. Oftentimes, your opponent will attempt to block the Lockdown by posting on his foot and keeping his knee off the mat. In such a scenario, utilizing this technique allows you to bring his knee down, get the Lockdown, and get to work. I've used this move for years, but this is the first time that I'm actually teaching it. It's such an important part of my game because when pulling half guard you need to establish some sort of clinch, and the Lockdown is an excellent place to start.

Einstein is on one knee, attempting to pass my guard. My goal is to force him into the Lockdown.

I bring my left foot to the inside of Einstein's right leg.

I hook my left foot around the back of Einstein's right ankle and wrap my left hand around the back of his right knee.

As I sit back, I force Einstein off balance by pulling his right knee into my body with my right hand and lifting his right leg up using my left hook on his foot.

Falling over to my right side, I continue to draw Einstein's right leg into me using my left hand.

Now that I have Einstein's right knee to the mat, I unhook my left foot and begin establishing the Lockdown.

I secure the Lockdown by hooking my left foot under my right leg, and then hooking my right foot under Einstein's right leg.

Butt Scoot Blast

This is another way to trap an opponent into your half guard. In this technique, you're going to scoot toward your opponent, hook your legs on the insides of his legs, transition to X-Guard, and then use your positioning to topple his base. Once you have caused him to fall forward, you can secure the Lockdown by forcing him to defend against a sweep. It's not a simple technique—you must have quick and precise leg work—but it's a good option to have in your arsenal.

Einstein is on his feet, trying to avoid getting caught in my guard.

Posting on my right hand, I scoot my butt forward to close the distance.

Still scooting forward, I hook my right foot around the back of Einstein's left knee.

Having closed the distance, I drop my body to the mat and wrap my left foot around the inside of Einstein's right leg.

MASTERING THE RUBBER GUARD

Using my left hook on Einstein's right leg, I spin my body in a counterclockwise direction and wrap my right arm around the inside of his left leg.

Continuing to rotate in a counterclockwise direction, I fall to my back and hook my right arm deeper around Einstein's left leg.

I grab Einstein's right ankle with my left hand. At the same time, I shoot my right foot up between his legs, hooking it around the inside of his right hip. This puts me in the X-Guard.

I destroy Einstein's base by pulling his left leg into me using my right hook and elevating my hips. This causes Einstein to fall forward.

As Einstein continues to fall forward, I hook my left arm over his right shoulder. At the same time, I drive his right leg upward with my left butterfly hook.

I hook my right foot underneath Einstein's right leg, which allows me to remove my left hook from his leg and begin securing the Lockdown.

Still elevating Einstein's right leg with my right foot, I hook my left leg over his right leg.

I hook my left foot underneath my right leg.

I extend my legs to secure the Lockdown.

Part Three
BUTTERFLY GUARD

Introduction to the Butterfly Guard

Because my half guard, butterfly guard, and Rubber Guard are all part of an elaborate system that leads you to the finish line, I am never weary of pulling guard. As a matter of fact, I'm always looking to pull guard, secure the Lockdown and the double under-hooks, and then whip up to my side. When I can achieve all three goals, my opponent is in serious trouble.

There is a group of black belts at the Machado Academy who understand just how dangerous my half guard can be. To avoid getting stuck in my half guard and spending precious energy trying to defend my various sweeps, their entire goal when we roll is to stop me from obtaining the Lockdown. That's their entire strategy, to prevent me from getting the Lockdown at all costs. They figure that if they can shut me down on that front, they can shut me down on all fronts.

I have to admit that it was quite frustrating when I first encountered this blockade, but it didn't take long for me to see the advantages. Having an opponent focus so intently on avoiding the Lockdown opens up other opportunities, such as securing an over-hook and an under-hook. Once I establish those hooks, I can usually swim my feet to the inside of my opponent's hips and secure my butterfly hooks. Instead of lying flat on my back, which offers no options at all, I force my opponent away from me using my legs. As my opponent sits back to reestablish his base, I squeeze my over-hook and under-hook tight and sit up with him, securing a control position I call the Cocoon.

The Cocoon

The Cocoon opens up all sorts of options. It allows you to execute a number of sweeps, including the Stick Shift and the Jean Jacques sweep to either the right side or left. You can either battle for the double under-hooks and go back to half guard or transition back to closed guard and start working your submissions. You can use repeated sweep attempts to create space between you and your opponent, which allows you to transition to full guard, the Pyramid, or X-Guard. As long as you are always thinking outside the box, you will never encounter a blockade that you can't get around.

The key to developing a powerful butterfly guard game is to really learn how to gain control of your opponent using an over-hook and an under-hook. Unlike in traditional Brazilian Jiu-Jitsu, there is no sleeve or collar to latch onto when no-gi grappling. All you have are those hooks. If you master them, a plethora of options become available to you. If you don't, you will get stuck lying flat on your back, which won't get you anywhere.

Butterfly Sweeps & Transitions

Jiu-jitsu practitioners who roll with a gi nail butterfly sweeps all the time in practice and competition. It's not that they're better at butterfly sweeps than practitioners who roll without a gi—it's just that they have all sorts of handles to latch onto. If you secure a tight over-hook on an opponent's arm and then latch onto his sleeve or collar, you can lock his arm in place. Sweeping him suddenly becomes a piece of cake because he can no longer post his arm to counter your sweep. You obviously don't have that option when grappling without a gi, which brings down the effectiveness of butterfly sweeps by at least fifty percent. Even though this is a harsh reality, butterfly sweeps can still be a powerful tool to the no-gi grappler. It takes a lot of energy to counter a sweep by posting, and if you go for one sweep attempt after another, eventually your opponent's defenses will start to drop.

Executing a butterfly sweep from the Cocoon position is also an excellent way to set up a transition. The instant your opponent posts his arm to counter your sweep, he opens a window for you to transition directly into full guard, the Pyramid, the Dogfight, X-Guard, or back to half guard where you can get the Lockdown. It is imperative that you become a master at making these transitions. They won't be easy at first, but after running through the scenario-based options I've laid out in the upcoming pages hundreds of times, you will develop the decision-making skills, flexibility, and quickness needed to capitalize on an opponent's counter to your sweep. Once you learn how to pounce on transition opportunities the moment they arise, your butterfly guard game just got a whole lot more dangerous.

Jean Jacques Sweep

As I mentioned in the introduction, sweeping an opponent from the butterfly guard can be a challenging task when grappling without a gi. With few handles to grab onto, it can be difficult to trap your opponent's arm, which makes it easy for him to counter your sweep by posting. Some no-gi sweeps work better than others to gain control of your opponent's arm, and the Jean Jacques is high on the list. Your opponent will still do his best to free his arm as you start casting him over, so it's key that you maintain a tight trap on his arm. You also want to follow him over. If you don't follow your opponent, you'll give him a chance to recover and scurry back into your guard.

The photographs below show how to secure the mount with this sweep, but you can just as easily transition into Twister Side Control by rolling all the way through. If you're unsuccessful with the sweep because your opponent finds a way to free his arm and stop the sweep by posting, don't get discouraged. You just opened a window of opportunity to transition to either the Half Guard or the Pyramid, which you will learn about shortly.

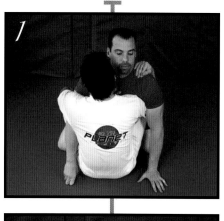

1

Sitting up in my butterfly guard, I have a right under-hook and a left over-hook. This is called the Cocoon, an ideal position for attacking your opponent.

2

Releasing my right under-hook, I slide my right hand down Laurence's back, underneath his armpit, and then place it on his left shoulder. Notice how my right elbow is locked tight to my side.

3

I slide my right hand down Laurence's left shoulder and establish a tight grip on his triceps. Notice how I've hooked Laurence's left arm with my forearm and the crook of my elbow.

Pulling my right elbow into my body, Laurence's left arm gets trapped between my arm and ribs. Once I have his arm locked tight, I begin to fall back onto the right side of my body.

Rolling further onto my right side, I push off the mat with my right foot and lift Laurence's right leg with my left foot. It is important to keep your right arm locked tight over your opponent's arm to prevent him from posting and countering the sweep.

I continue to sweep Laurence over by driving off my right foot and kicking his right leg up with my left foot. It is important to notice that I'm rolling onto my right shoulder and sweeping Laurence to my right side, not over my head.

Sweeping Laurence all the way over to his back, I land in the mount. I acquired this positioning by guiding his right leg all the way to the mat with my left foot. If I had launched him over and not followed, I would have given him space to scramble back into my guard.

Tucking my left knee underneath Laurence's right arm, I slide my left hand underneath his head and my right arm underneath his left arm. Clasping my hands together underneath his left shoulder using a Gable Grip, I secure the mount position.

Stick Shift

For those times when you execute the Jean Jacques Sweep and your opponent manages to free his arm and post, this is a great fail-safe technique to utilize. The moment your opponent posts, you want to slide your hand down to his wrist and pull his posted arm back in. It is important to do this quickly, as well as maintain upward pressure with your butterfly hook to prevent your opponent from reestablishing his base.

I've achieved the Cocoon position by sitting up in my butterfly guard and establishing a right under-hook and a left over-hook. I'm in the perfect position to execute the Jean Jacques Sweep.

Releasing my right under-hook, I slide my right hand down Laurence's back, underneath his armpit, and then place it on his left shoulder. Notice how my right elbow is locked tight to my side.

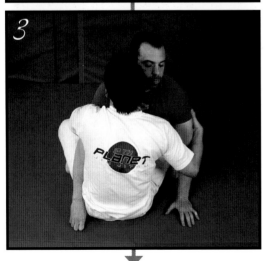

I slide my right hand down Laurence's left shoulder and establish a tight grip on his triceps. Notice how I've hooked Laurence's left arm with my forearm and the crook of my elbow.

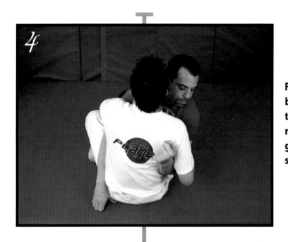

Pulling my right elbow into my body, Laurence's left arm gets trapped between my arm and ribs. With his arm secure, I begin to fall back onto the right side of my body.

Before I can execute the Jean Jacques Sweep, Laurence manages to free his left arm. He quickly posts it out to his left side, blocking my sweep.

Without hesitating, I quickly slide my right hand down to Laurence's wrist and establish a firm grip. It is important to continue to apply upward pressure with your left leg to keep the majority of your opponent's weight distributed on his posted arm. That way when you pull his posted arm back to your side, he will go right over.

Continuing to drive my left foot into the air, I drop my right foot to the mat and push off. As I do this, I pull Laurence's left arm into my side to collapse his base.

To sweep Laurence over, I continue to drive my left foot upward and push off the mat with my right leg. Notice how I am rolling onto my right shoulder and guiding Laurence's leg all the way over. That control is very important. If you try tossing your opponent, you may lose the top position in an ensuing scramble.

Because I have guided Laurence's leg all the way over, I land in the mount.

I slide my left arm underneath Laurence's head and clasp my hands together using a Gable Grip. I am now in the perfect position to launch a mount attack.

MASTERING THE RUBBER GUARD

Jean Jacques 2

The success rate of this sweep isn't nearly as high as the previous sweeps because you don't have your opponent's arm locked tight to your body. Unless you nail it with lightning fast quickness, your opponent will have an opportunity to post his arm. However, the success rate of this sweep improves greatly when you go for it off another sweep. For example, you attempt to sweep your opponent to your left using the Jean Jacques Sweep. Your opponent blocks the sweep by posting his arm, but before he can reestablish his base, you lock your over-hook tight and take him in the opposite direction with the Jean Jacques 2. When you're successful with this combination, you'll want to transition into side control instead of heading all the way over into the mount. The reason for this is because your under-hook will become an over-hook for your opponent, and he can use that over-hook to sweep you to your back. He can still acquire the over-hook when you land in side control, but it won't put you in nearly as much danger. (To have the most success with this technique, you want to lock your over-hook down slightly above your opponent's elbow. If you get much higher up than that, he'll have a much easier time posting his arm.)

I've achieved the Cocoon position by sitting up in my butterfly guard and establishing a right under-hook and a left over-hook. I'm in the perfect position to attack.

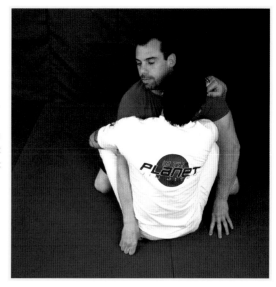

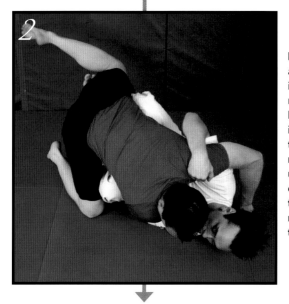

Keeping my over-hook as tight as possible, I suck my left elbow into my body. Immediately I roll onto my left shoulder, drive Laurence's left leg upward using my right butterfly hook, and turn Laurence's body in the direction of the sweep using my under-hook. It is important to execute all these steps simultaneously or your opponent will realize your intentions and try to counter.

Driving my left foot off the mat, I continue to sweep Laurence over by lifting his left leg with my right butterfly hook. As I do this, I use my right under-hook to help pin his shoulders to the mat. This hinders his ability to scramble to a more dominant position while I'm in the process of securing side control.

Instead of following Laurence over and claiming the mount, I twist my hips and slide my right leg underneath my posted left leg. It is important to notice how I am lifting Laurence's right arm so I can slide my right leg under his shoulder. This is an essential step when making the full transition into side control.

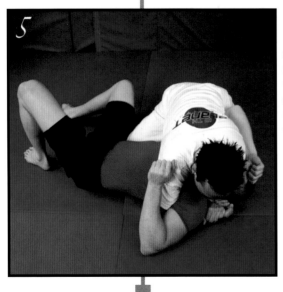

Still lifting up on Laurence's right arm, I rotate up to my knees. Then I slide my left arm underneath Laurence's head, clasp my hands together using a Gable Grip, and dig my knees deep into his side. I am now in side control, pinning Laurence's shoulders to the mat with an over/under body lock.

Cocoon to X-Guard Sweep

When you attempt a sweep from the butterfly position and your opponent posts his arm, you have a couple of different options. You can pull his arm back in using the Stick Shift or you can sweep him in the opposite direction using the previous technique. But not every opponent will respond to your sweep in the same way. Instead of posting out an arm, some jiu-jitsu practitioners will post out their leg. In such cases, I will immediately transition into the X-Guard Sweep. To make the most out of this technique, it is important that you sweep your opponent all the way over and then come up into side control. I see people get lazy with this all the time—they sweep their opponent and then just sit there. It gives their opponent a chance to scramble right back into their guard, where the battle starts all over again. I admit that it can be difficult sitting up into your opponent with this sweep, but the abdominal strength it requires is well worth the effort. After going through all that toil to roll your opponent over, you might as well put in the extra effort to ensure that you acquire a dominant position.

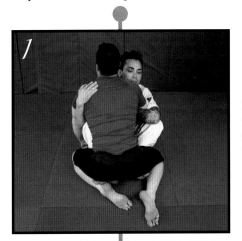

I've achieved the Cocoon position by sitting up in my butterfly guard and establishing a right under-hook and a left over-hook. I'm in the perfect position to attack.

Releasing my right under-hook, I slide my right hand down Laurence's back, underneath his armpit, and then place it on his left shoulder. Notice how my right elbow is locked tight to my side.

I slide my right hand down Laurence's left shoulder and establish a tight grip just above his elbow on his triceps.

Pulling my right elbow into my body, Laurence's left arm gets trapped between my arm and ribs. With his arm secure, I begin to fall back onto the right side of my body.

As I fall back onto my right shoulder, Laurence posts his left leg out and blocks the sweep.

Immediately I slip my right arm to the inside of Laurence's left arm, hook my right arm around his leg, and latch onto his knee with my right hand. I then use that hook to help me rotate in a counterclockwise direction. It is important to notice that I am keeping my left over-hook tight. This keeps Laurence from posturing up before I have a chance to transition into the X-Guard.

Still rotating in counterclockwise direction, I slide my right leg underneath Laurence's right leg and then hook my right foot around the outside of his right hip. This puts me in the X-Guard.

Releasing my left over-hook, I reach down and grab Laurence's right ankle with my left hand. Notice how my right foot is hooked high up on Laurence's hip, and my left foot is hooked just behind his knee. This is important because when I execute the sweep, I need to collapse his left leg. If both of my feet were high on Laurence's hip, he would still be able to maintain his base. With my current positioning, I am able to collapse his leg on three levels—the hip, the knee, and the ankle.

Pulling Laurence's left ankle toward my head, I straighten out my legs and collapse his base. Notice how I maintain control of Laurence's left leg with my under-hook. This keeps him from stepping back with his left leg and stopping the sweep. It is also important to notice I've secured my right under-hook just above his knee rather than down by his ankle. This gives me the optimum control over his leg and lowers his chances of freeing it.

As Laurence falls back to the mat, I immediately sit up with him so I can begin my transition into side control.

I continue to sit up, distributing my weight on my right leg.

Coming down on top of Laurence, I post my left leg out and distribute the majority of weight on my right knee, which is now digging into Laurence's belly. Sliding my left arm underneath Laurence's head, I clasp my hands together. I am now in the knee-on-belly side control position, pinning Laurence's shoulders to the mat with an over/under body lock.

Cocoon to Dogfight

Transitioning to the Dogfight position is another option you have from the butterfly guard. To set up the transition, you generally want to go for a couple of butterfly sweeps first. This not only gets your opponent thinking about sweeps rather than transitions, but it will also cause him to shift his weight back. Once his weight is back, you can sometimes pop right up into the Dogfight position. However, the transition should be done quickly because your opponent will most likely fall forward to close the distance and halt your transition.

I've achieved the Cocoon position by sitting up in my butterfly guard and establishing a right under-hook and a left over-hook. I'm in the perfect position to attack.

Releasing my under-hook, I turn to my right side and post my right hand on the mat behind me.

Releasing my over-hook, I slide my left arm under Laurence's right arm to secure an under-hook.

I reach my left hand around Laurence's back and latch onto his left hip. Applying downward pressure with my left arm and posting on my right elbow, I scoot my hips away from Laurence's body and step my left leg over the top of Laurence's right leg.

Laurence wraps his right arm over my left arm, giving him a Whizzer. To counter the power behind his over-hook, I drive into him with my under-hook. This allows me to quickly swing my hips behind his hips and start coming up to my knees. If Laurence hadn't wrapped his right arm over my left, I could have slipped my body underneath his arm and taken his back.

Still driving into Laurence with my under-hook, I come all the way up to my knees, slip my left leg underneath his right leg, and sit back. This puts me into the Dogfight position, from which I have a number of options.

Cocoon to Pyramid

If an opponent counters the Jean Jacques sweep by posting his arm, a good option is to immediately transition into a Rubber Guard position called the Pyramid. The transition begins much like the Stick Shift in that you slide your hand down to the wrist of your opponent's posted arm. However, instead of pulling his arm back into your side so you can continue the sweep, you want to use your grip to keep his arm posted away from you. This buys you the time and space needed to bring your legs up and establish the Pyramid position. Sometimes it will even buy you enough time and space to lock in the Triangle.

Because we spend so much time drilling at my Academy, my students come up with options like 'Cocoon to Pyramid' on a regular basis. We work tirelessly on stringing techniques together because that is the only way you will catch many opponents. If you manage to roll an opponent with a sweep, the chances are he will go out and learn the counter. The next time you try to use that sweep, he will know exactly what you are trying to achieve and shut you down. But if you follow up with another attack based upon his new positioning, you can leave him in the dust. Drilling techniques back to back is imperative for developing a dangerous game.

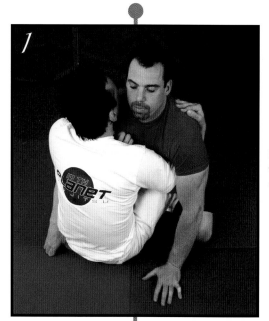

I've achieved the Cocoon position by sitting up in my butterfly guard and establishing a right under-hook and a left over-hook. I'm in the perfect position to attack.

Releasing my right under-hook, I slide my right hand down Laurence's back, underneath his armpit, and then place it on his left shoulder. Notice how my right elbow is locked tight to my side.

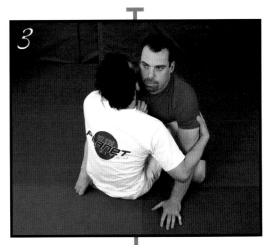

I slide my right hand down Laurence's left shoulder and establish a tight grip on his triceps.

Pulling my right elbow into my body, Laurence's left arm gets trapped between my arm and ribs. With his arm secure, I begin to fall back onto the right side of my body.

Before I can complete my sweep, Laurence manages to free his left arm. He quickly posts it out to his left side, blocking my sweep.

Without hesitating, I quickly slide my right hand down to Laurence's wrist and establish a firm grip.

The moment I have a firm grasp on Laurence's wrist, I release my left butterfly hook and swing my left leg out from underneath him. It is important that you keep your over-hook tight because once your opponent feels you release your butterfly hook, he will want to sit back to regain his posture. As long as you control his arm with a tight over-hook, it will make it very difficult for him to achieve this.

Still controlling Laurence's left wrist with my right hand, I swing my left leg around to the back of his head. As I do this, I start pulling my right knee up toward the front of Laurence's left shoulder.

To secure the Pyramid position, I slide my right knee all the way in front of Laurence's left shoulder and then squeeze my knees together. From here it is important to maintain control of your opponent's wrist because it allows you to set up a Triangle. You also want to keep your opponent's right hand pinned to the mat, which can be achieved by really clamping down on his arm with your left over-hook. To learn about your options from here, visit the Pyramid Section.

Part Four
Rubber Guard

Introduction to the Rubber Guard

PRIMARY PATH OF THE RUBBER GUARD

    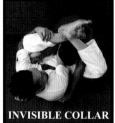 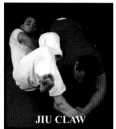

	MISSION CONTROL	NEW YORK	CHILL DOG	INVISIBLE COLLAR	JIU CLAW
LEVEL ONE	**LEVEL TWO**	**LEVEL THREE**	**LEVEL FOUR**	**LEVEL FIVE**	**LEVEL SIX**
Breaking Opponent Down	Keeping Opponent Broken Down/Freeing up an Arm to Work	Trapping Opponent's Hand to the Mat	Clearing Opponent's Neck	Testing out the Invisible Collar Submission	Transitioning to the Omaplata Position

I often refer to the Rubber Guard as an elaborate video game that starts the moment you pull an opponent into your guard. The more time you spend with this game, the better you get at progressing upward through the levels. But just like with any video game, getting started can often be frustrating because you don't understand how to use the tools at your disposal to complete your goals. To keep you from wandering in confusion, I have included the entire players manual in the upcoming pages.

To get the most out of this manual, you should start by learning how to accomplish the primary goal of level one, which is to pull your opponent from the sitting position down into the clinch. I refer to this as 'breaking your opponent down.' If your opponent is sitting up in your guard and you are lying flat on your back, he has all sorts of options and you have none. There are several ways to pull your opponent down into the clinch, and the various options I give you in the upcoming section should be drilled over and over. It might seem tedious, but you need to be able to establish a clinching position with your opponent while in the guard otherwise you will never make it to the higher levels where all the really cool stuff happens. Breaking your opponent down into the clinch is the heart of the Rubber Guard system because it takes you places.

Once you've broken an opponent down into your guard, you must then learn how to keep him broken down. One of the most common ways to achieve this is by clamping your legs tightly around your opponent's body and wrapping both arms around his head. It is an excellent way to keep your opponent's posture broken down, but with all of your limbs tied up, it offers very little in the way of offense.

To solve this dilemma, I developed Mission Control. To achieve this position after breaking an opponent down, you bring one of your legs high up on your opponent's back, wrap it over his shoulder, and then lock your leg in place by hooking your opposite wrist around your ankle. This frees up one of your arms, which is absolutely huge. It's huge because it allows you to maintain control of your opponent and still be offensive.

From Mission Control, the next step is to force your opponent's hand to the mat using your free arm. If you don't get your opponent's hand to the mat, you won't be able to reach Chill Dog and make use of all its options, including the Invisible Collar, and you certainly won't be able to reach Jiu-Claw and make use of its options, including the Omaplata. Sometimes getting your opponent's hand to the mat can be just as difficult as breaking your opponent down, so I will give you multiple techniques to achieve your goal. But other times your opponent will make a mistake and put his hands on the mat as you break him down. For this reason, you must always ask yourself a very simple question when you reach Mission Control—What are my opponent's hands doing? Are his hands on my chest? Are they on the mat? Does he have one hand on my chest and one hand on the mat? If your opponent puts a hand on the mat and you are slow to realize this, then you are giving him an opportunity to correct his mistake. You can still utilize Mission Control, Retard Control, or Crack Head Control and work to get his hand to the mat, but you could have bypassed all those steps if you had been paying attention to the positioning of his hands.

Trapping your opponent's hand to the mat puts you in the New York control position, which is level three. From New York you're going to work to move the arm you have hooked around your ankle to the other side of your opponent's head, and then dig your forearm into his neck. I refer to this as 'clearing your opponent's neck,' and I will give you numerous ways to accomplish this task. Once you do this, you will be on level four, which is Chill dog. Edging in on the finish line, things really start to get fun. From Chill Dog I will show you how to slap on the Invisible Collar submission, as well as show you how to make the transition from Chill Dog to Jiu-Claw if the Invisible Collar doesn't work. Then from Jiu-Claw I will show you multiple ways to finish the game or start a whole new video game by sweeping your opponent over into Twister Side Control.

This is the main route that you will take to the finish line. If your opponent makes a mistake while you're traveling this primary path, I will give you several ways to apply a submission and reach the finish line early. I will show you how to get around almost every blockade your opponent can throw at you. I will also give you cheat codes that allow you to jump back and forth between the various Rubber Guard control positions, as well as between the Rubber Guard and both the half guard and butterfly guard. The trick to mastering the Rubber Guard is to become so familiar with the steps that they become instinctual. You want to get to the point where you capitalize on opportunities before you even have time to think.

Troubleshooting Mission Control

A lot of jiu-jitsu practitioners tell me that when they utilize Mission Control, their opponents keep stepping over their free leg and passing their guard. The reason for this is simple—they aren't squeezing their knees together hard enough. To get really efficient at Mission Control, you always have to be practicing that squeeze. If you don't get accustomed to controlling your opponent with the squeeze in Mission Control, you're not going to reach New York or Chill Dog. It is important to remember that my system is like a video game. You have to master one level before you can move onto the next.

Don't get discouraged if it doesn't come overnight—it took me years to master. It takes time to develop the gas and endurance needed to pull this system off because you're working off the clinch. I have noticed that jiu-jitsu practitioners who are used to grappling with a gi have a particularly difficult time with this. In the gi game it's all about yanking and pulling rather than clinching and squeezing. As I mentioned in the beginning of the book, the way you control your opponent in traditional jiu-jitsu versus no-gi grappling is so different that it almost makes them two separate sports.

Retard and Crack Head Control

RETARD CONTROL   CRACK HEAD CONTROL

After breaking an opponent down into your guard, Mission Control is an excellent position to go to because it allows you to maintain control over your opponent while at the same time free up an arm so you can work to get his hand to the mat. However, Mission Control can sometimes be hard to maintain on an opponent who is strong and full of energy. If your opponent is thrashing with all of his might to posture back up, a much safer position to head to is Retard Control.

To transition to Retard Control from Mission Control, all you have to do is form a Gable Grip with your hands around the ankle that you brought up toward your opponent's head. Clamping down tight does wonders to lock your opponent's shoulders. I call it Retard Control because if your opponent has retard strength, you need to use this position to calm him down. Although the position doesn't allow you to work like Mission Control because you have both hands tied up, it makes it very hard for your opponent to posture back up in your guard.

If your opponent's elbows are tucked tightly together on top of your chest when you establish Retard Control, you can transition back to Mission Control and go for the Arm Bar. If your opponent's hands are on your chest but his elbows are angled out, you can go back to Mission Control to execute The Zombie and get his hand to the mat. If your opponent is still going nuts when you get him Retard Control, doing everything in his power to regain his posture, you can transition into Crack Head Control by bringing your other leg up into the mix and using it to help hold your opponent's shoulders down. The majority of the time this is a sure-fire way to get your opponent to chill out.

From Crack Head Control you have a few more options than in Retard Control because you are freeing up one of your hands. You can go directly to The Zombie and get your opponent's hand to the mat. If The Zombie doesn't work because your opponent is keen to the Rubber Guard game, then you can execute The Pump, which leads to the Spider Web position and a submission. The only negative part about Crack Head Control is that you have to take both of your feet off of your opponent's hips, which makes it easier for him to stand up and stack you by driving his weight down. For this reason, you don't want to hang out in Crack Head Control all day long. You want to make a move.

These three positions—Mission Control, Retard Control, and Crack Head Control—should be viewed as tools that allow you to reach more advantageous positions such as New York, Chill Dog, and Jiu-Claw. Sometimes you will need to use Crack Head Control to get to those levels, sometimes you will need to use Mission Control, and sometimes you will need to use all three. It all depends upon your opponent's reactions when you break his posture down. The trick is to not only become a master at flowing back and forth between these positions, but also learning when to make these transitions. I would like to tell you this comes overnight, but it takes time.

Pyramid

E very once in a while you'll go up against an opponent who stops every attempt you make to get his hand to the mat from Mission Control. The Exhumer, The Night of the Living Dead, The Zombie—nothing is working for you. The Pump isn't working for you. In such cases, you always have the option to release Mission Control and go

back to regular full guard. From there, you can establish your butterfly hooks and start working your sweeps. If your opponent doesn't take his hands off your chest, you'll most likely get the sweep. If he posts his arms to stop the sweep, it gives you the space you need to transition to a Rubber Guard position I call the Pyramid.

In the butterfly section of this book, I already showed you how to go from the butterfly guard to the Pyramid. In this section, I will show you how to transition from Mission Control to the Pyramid. There are just a few added steps, but you must become efficient at making the transition because the Pyramid opens up so many options.

The key to making the most out of the Pyramid is to learn how to maintain control of your opponent. You won't be grabbing your ankle to keep his posture broken, so you must develop two things—a very tight over-hook, and a strong leg curl to keep your opponent's shoulders down. Once you develop this control, you then have to learn how to get your knee in front of your opponent's shoulder like you did with the Stick Shift technique in the butterfly section. This lands you in the Pyramid, and from there it's just a few small movements to lock in a Triangle.

It can sometimes be hard to get your knee in front of your opponent's shoulder, but learning how to control your opponent's wrist like you did with the Stick Shift will improve your percentages. If you aren't able to get your knee in front of your opponent's shoulder because he is hugging your knee or fighting your wrist control, your options just narrowed. I will give you multiple techniques to deal with such a scenario, but if they all fail, a good option is to execute the Kung Fu Move and transition straight to the Jiu-Claw control position.

Non-Stop

The Non-Stop is one of the better techniques that you can use to break an opponent down into your guard. When executing this move, you always want to be conscious of whether or not your opponent puts his hands on the mat. If he is smart and doesn't drop a hand, you're going to have to force his hand to the mat using one of the upcoming techniques. But if he does, you should immediately capitalize on the opportunity. Instead of having to assume Mission Control and then utilize The Zombie, Night of the Living Dead, or the Exhumer, you can transition right into New York. A lot of times your opponent will put a hand on the mat, realize his mistake, and then quickly place it on your chest. If you allow such a thing to happen, then you just missed out on a golden opportunity. Heading into this technique expecting that your opponent will make a mistake can allow you to cut some serious corners.

Laurence is postured up in my closed guard. In order to attack, I first have to break him down into my guard.

I open my guard by uncrossing my legs, and then I sit up into Laurence.

Sitting all the way up, I wrap my left arm all the way around the back of Laurence's head and grab my right biceps.

Squeezing my arms together to keep Laurence tight against my body, I break his posture by pulling him down into my guard. Immediately I notice that his right arm is on the mat. Before Laurence can realize he's made a terrible mistake, I will capitalize on the opportunity and trap his hand to the mat.

To trap Laurence's hand to the mat, I bring my left leg up and wrap my left arm around the outside of my knee. At the same time, I post my right foot on Laurence's left hip and shove his base back, making it even harder for him to sit back up and reclaim his posture.

I wrap my left arm tightly around my left knee, and then I hook my right wrist over my left ankle. Once I lock everything tight, I've secured New York. From here I can either attempt a finish or work to bring my right arm to the right side of Laurence's head, which would land me in Chill Dog.

Breaking an Opponent Down Into Mission Control

The majority of jiu-jitsu players know not to put their hand on the mat when you break them down into your guard, but a lot of times your opponent will be so consumed with maintaining his posture, he will drop his hands to the mat without thinking. If you jump on the opportunity, you can transition right into New York. That's the best possible scenario, but it doesn't always go down like that. If your opponent has tight defense and he keeps his hands planted firmly on your chest, you're going to have to assume Mission Control and then work to get his hand to the mat using one or more of the upcoming techniques.

Laurence is postured up in my closed guard. In order to attack, I first have to break him down into my guard.

Opening my guard and posting on my right elbow, I sit up into Laurence.

Sitting all the way up, I wrap both of my arms around Laurence and clasp my hands together behind his back using a Gable Grip.

I break Laurence's posture by pulling him down into my guard. Instead of placing his hands on the mat, Laurence places both hands on my chest. With his defense strong, I will need to transition to Mission Control and work to trap his hand to the mat.

I place my right foot on Laurence's left hip. To transition to Mission Control, I drive Laurence's hips back with my right foot, bring my left foot up to the back of his head, and then wrap my right wrist around my left ankle. Now that I'm in Mission Control, I have several options to get his hand to the mat, which will be my next goal.

Over/Under-Hook

Another way to break your opponent's posture while in the guard is to sit up, secure an over-hook and an under-hook with your arms, and then pull him down. However, this can be a difficult task to accomplish when grappling with an opponent who is good at driving your hips down every time you attempt to sit up. The best way to counter this defense is to sit up to your side. If you still encounter a battle, try throwing one of the other posture breaking techniques at your opponent first. This will usually steal some of his focus, making it much easier to secure a tight over-hook and under-hook. Combinations are key when grappling with an opponent who has tight defense.

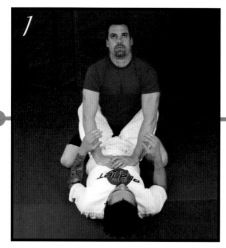

Laurence is postured up in my closed guard. In order to attack, I first have to break him down into my guard.

Opening my guard, I post on my right hand and scoot my hips slightly out to my left. As I do this, I reach my left arm underneath Laurence's right arm for an under-hook.

Sitting all the way up, I slip my left arm all the way underneath Laurence's right arm, wrap my right arm around his left arm, and then clasp my hands together behind his back using a Gable Grip.

I break Laurence's posture by pulling him down into my guard. Because he didn't make the mistake of putting his hands on the mat, I need to immediately transition to Mission Control and start working to get his hand to the mat.

S-grip

As promised, I'm giving you multiple options to break your opponent down into your guard. This particular technique works well on an opponent who prevents you from sitting up by driving your hips down into the mat. To execute this move, all you have to do is sit far enough up to clasp your hands together behind your opponent's head using an S-grip. If you can get the S-grip but you still can't break your opponent's posture, let go and move onto something else. Some guys are just too strong to catch with this technique, and you will waste energy trying to fight them.

Laurence is postured up in my closed guard. In order to attack, I first have to break him down into my guard.

I open my guard and sit up into Laurence.

Understanding my intentions, Laurence stops me from sitting all the way up by posting his hands on my hips and driving them into the mat. However, I've managed to sit far enough up to wrap both hands around the back of his neck and lock my hands together using an S-grip.

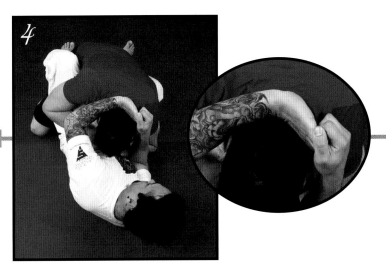

As I fall back, I pull Laurence into me and drive my right elbow toward the mat.

Now that I have broken Laurence's posture by pulling him down into my guard, I lock my feet together and establish a closed guard. I also have room to switch my S-grip to a Gable Grip, which allows me to lock my arms tightly around his head. From here I will immediately work to get Laurence into Mission Control.

Double Under-Hooks

When you use the double under-hooks to break an opponent's posture, you will force his arms to the outside of your hips, which means there is a good change he will place his hands on the mat when you pull him down into your guard. This allows you to either trap his hand to the mat and move into New York or use your under-hooks to help lock his shoulder and transition into an Arm Bar. Just like the over/under hooks, this technique works great on an opponent who is driving your hips down into the mat to prevent you from sitting up.

Laurence is postured up in my closed guard. In order to attack, I first have to break him down into my guard.

I open my guard and sit up into Laurence. In an attempt to prevent me from sitting all the way up, he drives his hands down into my hips. To relieve that pressure, I drive my left arm underneath his right arm, as well as drive my right arm underneath his left arm. This pushes his hands to the outside of my hips and allows me to sit all the way up.

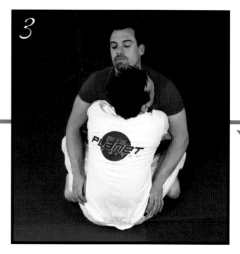

Sitting all the way up, I wrap both of my arms around Laurence and lock my hands together behind his back using a Gable Grip.

I break Laurence's posture by pulling him down into my guard. If Laurence tries to wedge his arms onto my chest, I can work to lock one of his shoulders with a leg, which would allow me to execute an Arm Bar. If he doesn't make such an attempt, I will work to establish an over-hook on one of his arms, which would allow me to trap his hand to the mat and obtain New York.

The Zombie

This technique comes in handy when you break an opponent down into your guard and he plants his hands on your chest. When this happens, it is important to notice the positioning of his elbows. If his elbows are tucked tightly together, you'll have the option of bringing your legs up and going for an Arm Bar. If his hands are on your chest but his elbows are angled out, you'll have a difficult time bringing up your legs. In such a scenario, a much better approach is to force your opponent's hand to the mat by utilizing The Zombie. Although it's not a finish, it puts you in New York, which allows you to transition to a more advantageous position.

After breaking Laurence down into Mission Control, I made the transition to Retard Control by locking my hands together on top of my left ankle using a Gable Grip. As long as I keep my arms locked tight, Laurence will have a very difficult time posturing back up. This gives me a few moments to survey my options. Immediately I spot Laurence's elbows hanging over the sides of my body, which will allow me to execute The Zombie.

I release Retard Control and retreat back into Mission Control. Notice how I am moving my left hand toward Laurence's right elbow.

I slip my left hand into the small gap between Laurence's right elbow and my body.

Once my left hand is through the gap, I straighten my arm upwards. This movement further separates Laurence's right arm from his body.

After straitening my left arm, I circle it around my left knee. Notice how this drives Laurence's right arm toward the mat.

Wrapping my left arm around my left knee, I secure New York. Notice how tightly I'm hugging my left knee—my left shoulder and left knee are actually being drawn together. This is very important because it gives Laurence no room to pull his arm out. Now I can start working for the Chill Dog Control position.

Night of the Living Dead

If your opponent understands the Rubber Guard system and defends all your attempts to get his hand to the mat, sometimes you have to resort to trickery to catch him. That is what Night of the Living dead is based upon. Instead of focusing on the arm you want to trap to the mat, you attack the opposite side of your opponent's body, leading him to believe that you have given up on trying to reach your goal. The moment he takes the bait and removes his arm from your chest, you want to immediately trap his hand to the mat and transition to New York.

After breaking Laurence down into Mission Control, I transitioned to Retard Control to keep him from posturing back up. I achieved this by locking my hands together on top of my left ankle using a Gable Grip.

I transition back to Mission Control with the intentions of getting Laurence's hand to the mat utilizing The Zombie. Because Laurence understands the Rubber Guard system, he senses The Zombie coming and keeps his right arm pressed tight against my body. With The Zombie shut down, I decide to utilize The Night of the Living Dead.

Immediately I reach my left arm across my body and over the top of my left foot. To lock my left arm in place, I latch onto my right wrist with my left hand.

Now that I'm attacking Laurence's left side, his main concern is to get his head back to the center of my chest because it offers the best defense. The moment Laurence grabs my right shoulder to help align his head with my body, I hook my right wrist around my left foot to reestablish Mission Control and quickly swing my left arm towards the back of my left knee, which moves me closer to New York.

Wrapping my left arm around my left knee, I trap Laurence's hand to the mat and establish New York. Notice how tightly I'm hugging my left knee—my left shoulder and left knee are actually being drawn together. This is very important because it gives Laurence no room to pull his arm out. I can now start working for the Chill Dog control position.

The Exhumer

This is a good way to get your opponent's hand to the mat when nothing else is working. From Mission Control, I'll slide one of my forearms across the back of my opponent's neck, form a Gable Grip with my hands, and then squeeze my arms as tightly as I can. As the blade of my forearm drives into the back of my opponent's head, his face gets buried in my chest. The technique can cause your opponent quite a bit of pain, and the only way for him to relieve the pressure is to plant his hands on the mat and posture up. The moment he does this, you want to trap his hand to the mat and transition to New York. The trick to mastering this technique is to develop a powerful squeeze. I have a damn good squeeze, and the move works for me about thirty percent of the time, which should be considered a high success rate.

I've broken Laurence down into Retard Control.

I transition to Mission Control with the intentions of getting Laurence's hand to the mat utilizing the Zombie, but Laurence keeps his elbow pressed tightly against my side.

Knowing Laurence won't let me execute the Zombie, I release Mission Control and wrap my left arm around the back of his head. Clasping my hands together using a Gable Grip, I squeeze my arms in tight. This buries his face into my chest and causes him a fair amount of pain. To alleviate some of that pain, Laurence pulls his right arm off of my chest with the intentions of using it to posture up.

I trap Laurence's right hand to the mat by wrapping my left arm around my left knee.

I secure New York by hooking my right wrist over my left leg. Now I will begin my transition to Chill Dog.

Mission Pump

A lot of times when you trap an opponent in Mission Control he will push off your chest with his hands in an effort to back out and escape. This is the perfect opportunity to execute The Mission Pump, which takes you to the Spider Web position.

I've broken Laurence down into Mission Control.

Laurence attempts to back out of Mission Control by pushing off my chest with both of his hands.

Rather than resisting, I release Mission Control and push off Laurence's left hip with my right foot, which helps me spin my hips in a counterclockwise direction. As I do this, I slide my left arm over Laurence's right arm and underneath his left arm. To keep his right arm trapped against my chest, I grab hold of my right hip with my left hand. This puts me in a position to attack. It is very important, however, that you continue to squeeze your knees together and apply downward pressure with your left leg. This keeps everything nice and tight. If you let up on that pressure, your opponent will be able to power out and posture up.

I hook my right arm around the inside of Laurence's left leg, and then use that hook to aid my counter-clockwise rotation. Notice how this puts my body at a forty-five degree angle with Laurence's body, which allows me to attack his right arm. However, in order to be able to attack that arm you must keep your left arm stretched tight across your body. If you don't, your opponent will be able to pull his arm free before you can bring your left leg to the left side of his head.

I wrap my left leg around the left side of Laurence's head.

To sweep Laurence over to his back, I apply downward pressure with both legs. My left leg drives into the side of Laurence's head, and my right leg drives into his left side. To help cast him over, I also C-cup my right hand around the inside of his left knee and push his leg upward. When done right, your opponent won't be able to resist the roll.

I maintain control of Laurence's body as he rolls over onto his back by squeezing my knees together, curling my legs tight over his body and head, and keeping my deep hook on his right arm super tight.

Without hesitating, I wrap my right arm around Laurence's right leg to prevent a scramble. I now have Laurence in the Spider Web position, which opens up all sorts of attacks. To learn your options, visit the Spider Web section.

Meat Hook to Triangle

Whenever I secure an opponent in my guard, I know exactly what I have to do. First I have to break him down, and then I have to get his hand to the mat. But when going up against one of my students or someone familiar with my Rubber Guard system, this can be difficult to accomplish. They know not to put their hand to the mat because I will get New York. They know if they keep their hands on my chest but their elbows are spread too far to the outside, I will get their hand to the mat using The Zombie. They know if they have their hands on my chest but their elbows are too close together, I will execute The Pump, which allows me to lock their shoulder and go for an Arm Bar. Against guys like this—guys who understand the Rubber Guard System and defend perfectly—transitioning from Mission Control to the Meat Hook and then slapping on a Triangle is a great option. Instead of taking the traditional route to Chill Dog or the Invisible Collar, you're ending the fight right off Mission Control with a submission.

I've broken Laurence down into Mission Control. He is defending well, so instead of trying to trap his hand to the mat, I decide to finish him off with the Meat Hook to Triangle.

Releasing Mission Control, I wrap my left arm over the top of my left foot. To secure my new positioning and make it hard for Laurence to posture up, I grab my right wrist with my left hand.

With Laurence no longer fighting to posture up, I grab his left shoulder with my left hand and slide my right arm underneath his left arm. Notice how this allows me to create separation between his left arm and his body.

Pushing Laurence's left elbow away from his body with my right arm, I create enough separation to pull my right knee up to the front of his left shoulder.

Sliding my right hand down Laurence's left arm, I latch onto his wrist and force his arm away from our bodies. Notice how I'm still locking my left leg tight over Laurence's right shoulder. This is very important because it stops Laurence from being able to posture back up and escape my submission attempt.

Still pushing Laurence's left arm away from our bodies using my right hand, I create enough space to bring my right leg out from underneath his left arm.

MASTERING THE RUBBER GUARD

Continuing to control Laurence's left arm with my right hand, I swing my right leg over his shoulder and grab just above my ankle with my left hand.

To establish the Triangle, I use my left hand to drag my right leg underneath my left knee. Once I've accomplished this, I curl my legs downward to apply pressure to the lock.

I secure the Triangle choke by pulling down on Laurence's head with both hands, curling my left leg down onto my right, and squeezing my knees together.

The Duda

In order to execute The Zombie from Mission Control and get your opponent's hand to the mat, you must swim your arm underneath your opponent's arm. Sometimes while you are in the process of doing this, your opponent realizes your intentions and clamps down before you can get your arm all the way through. This makes The Zombie hard to finish, but it sets you up perfectly for The Duda. The only downside to this move is that it ties up both of your arms, which makes it difficult to stop your opponent from standing up. If you go for this move in mixed martial arts competition and your opponent stands up, you might want to abandon the technique because your opponent will have the ability to stomp on your head.

After breaking Laurence down into Mission Control, I transitioned to Retard Control to keep him from posturing back up. I achieved this by locking my hands together on top of my left ankle using a Gable Grip.

I transition back to Mission Control with the intentions of getting Laurence's hand to the mat utilizing The Zombie. Keeping my right wrist locked tightly over my left leg, I attempt to slip my hand underneath Laurence's right arm.

As I reach my left hand underneath Laurence's right arm, he realizes my intentions and locks his arm tight to his body, trapping my arm before I can push it all the way through. Unless Laurence releases my trapped arm, The Zombie will be very hard to execute. Instantly I make the decision to transition to The Duda.

Releasing Mission Control, I grab Laurence's right wrist with my right hand and drive his arm down toward my hips. At the same time, I push my right foot off his left hip, which allows me to rotate my body in a clockwise direction.

Still rotating in a clockwise direction and driving Laurence's right wrist toward my hips, I swing my right leg around to the right side of Laurence's head. As I do this, I apply downward pressure with my left leg to prevent Laurence from posturing up.

I throw my right leg over the top of my left foot. To lock in the submission, I curl both of my legs down, elevate my hips, and pull my arms toward my head. Notice how the thumb of my left hand is pointed down. This allows me to dig my wrist bone into Laurence's arm. If your palm is flat on your chest, you may not inflict enough pain to cause your opponent to tap.

Crocodile

This is yet another technique you can utilize when an opponent keeps his arms tight, preventing you from getting his hand to the mat. Instead of trying to slide your hand underneath his elbow as you do with The Zombie, you force one of his arms toward the center of your chest by bashing your leg into his elbow. This sets you up for the Arm Bar, but it's very important to first trap your opponent's shoulder and switch the positioning of your legs. Once you've accomplished both tasks, the submission will be yours for the taking. If it should fail for whatever reason, you might want to transition back to Mission Control and immediately retry The Zombie. Oftentimes throwing several techniques in a row at an opponent will break down his defenses.

After breaking Laurence down into Mission Control, I transitioned to Retard Control to keep him from posturing back up. I achieved this by locking my hands together on top of my left ankle using a Gable Grip.

I transition back to Mission Control with the intentions of executing The Zombie, but instantly Laurence locks his elbow tight to my body. Instead of trying to force The Zombie, I decide to execute the Crocodile. I start the move by reaching my left arm over Laurence's right arm and grabbing hold of his left wrist with my left hand.

Keeping my grip on Laurence's left wrist tight, I swing my right leg to the outside of our bodies.

To force Laurence's left arm across my chest, I do two things at once. I pull on his left wrist with my left hand, and I drive my right leg into his left elbow. This sets me up for the Arm Bar.

I force Laurence's body forward by pulling my left leg down into the back of his head using my right hand. Then I throw my right leg over my left foot. It is important to notice that I am still pulling Laurence's left arm to my left side.

In order to apply the Arm Bar, I first need to lock Laurence's left shoulder. I do this by circling my right foot behind my left foot. Once I complete this motion, I squeeze my legs downward. If you don't maintain control of your opponent with your legs, he might be able to pull his trapped arm free and escape the submission.

Letting go of my left leg, I grab hold of Laurence's left wrist with my right hand. It is important to notice that I've kept Laurence's left shoulder locked with my right leg.

I maneuver my right leg to the left side of Laurence's head. To lock in the submission, I apply downward pressure with my legs, elevate my hips, and pull his left arm toward my chest with both hands.

The Pump

After running through a training partner again and again using Rubber Guard techniques, there will come a time when his defenses improve. He will learn how to position his elbows just right. He'll stop you from getting his hand to the mat, and he'll stop you from forcing one of his elbows across your chest with your usual techniques. When going up against such an opponent, a good option is to abandon your traditional pathway and concentrate on locking his arm. This can be done by transitioning from Mission Control to Crack Head Control and executing The Pump, a technique designed to force even the strongest of opponent's elbow to the inside so you can move into the Spider Web position and attack his arm.

After breaking Laurence down into Mission Control, I transitioned to Retard Control to keep him from posturing back up. I achieved this by locking my hands together on top of my left ankle using a Gable Grip.

Releasing Retard Control, I push my right foot off Laurence's left hip. This gives me the momentum to swing my right leg up toward my left foot.

With my right wrist still wrapped over my left ankle, I hook my right foot on top of my left foot. This lands me in Crack Head Control.

I place my left hand on Laurence's right elbow, pump my hips into him to create space, and then shove his arm between my legs.

Now that I've shoved Laurence's elbow between my legs, I squeeze my knees together and elevate my hips. My actions trap Laurence's right arm between my legs, which sets me up for the Arm Bar.

I slide my left arm over Laurence's right arm and trap it against my chest.

Hooking my left arm deeper over Laurence's right arm, I move closer to the Arm Bar.

Unlocking my feet and pulling my right arm down to the mat, I squeeze my knees together, elevate my hips, and curl legs down to lock Laurence's shoulders.

Twisting my hips in a counterclockwise direction, I hook my right hand around the inside of Laurence's left leg.

10

Using my right under-hook and my legs, I continue to rotate in a counterclockwise direction. This puts my body at a forty-five degree angle with Laurence and allows me to attack his arm. While making this transition, it is very important to maintain downward pressure with your legs to prevent your opponent from posturing up.

11

Hooking my left leg around the left side of Laurence's head, I can now force him over to his back.

12

Curling my legs downward, I C-cup Laurence's left leg with my right hand and then drive his leg over into the roll.

13

As Laurence rolls over onto his back, I hook my feet together. Notice how I am still controlling his left leg with my right hand. This helps to prevent him from scrambling for a more superior position.

14

I quickly wrap my right arm around the outside of Laurence's right leg to keep him trapped in the Spider Web position. From here, I have many submission opportunities, many of which are presented in the Spider Web section later in the book.

Mission Control to Pyramid

I've given you a lot of options from Mission Control—The Night of the Living Dead, The Zombie, and The Pump. Although most of these are high percentage moves, they become even more effective when utilized in combinations. But every once in a while you will go up against an opponent who manages to shut all these options down no matter how you throw them at him. In such a situation, a good option is to transition from Mission Control back to full guard, get your butterfly hooks in, and then start working your sweeps. Either your opponent will go over or he will post his arm on the mat to prevent the sweep. If your opponent posts, you have a small window to transition into the Pyramid. It's not a simple transition, but it can come in very handy with opponents who are familiar with the Rubber Guard and have worked on their defense. The Pyramid is a dead zone—once you've got it, the chances are high that you'll get either the Triangle or the Omaplata. But in order to reach the submission, you must first master this transition.

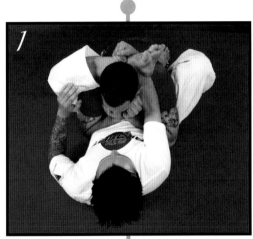

I've got Compella in Mission Control.

I attempt to get Compella's hand to the mat utilizing the Zombie, but his defense is tight.

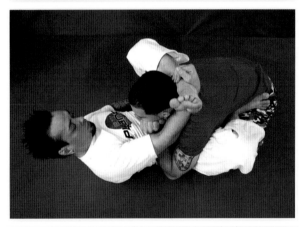

I immediately start the transition to Crack Head Control by bringing my right leg up.

I establish Crack Head Control by hooking my right foot over my left foot.

I attempt to punch Compella's right elbow toward the center of my chest, but once again his defense is too tight.

I have no choice but to abandon the Rubber Guard and retreat to full guard. However, it is important to notice that I am keeping Einstein's posture broken down by clasping my hands together behind his head.

Unhooking my feet, I post on my right elbow and come up onto my right side. As I do this, I hook my left arm over Compella's back and latch onto his left side with my hand.

I force a butterfly hook by slipping my right foot to the inside of Compella's left hip.

Driving upward with my right butterfly hook and pulling Compella to my left with my left hand, I slip my left foot to the inside of his right hip to establish my second butterfly hook.

I extend my legs and establish a left overhook on Compella's right arm.

I lift up with my left butterfly hook and push Compella's left elbow toward my legs with my right hand.

Compella posts his left arm to prevent being swept.

I slide my right hand down Compella's arm and latch onto his wrist.

I lift my left leg and bring my right knee to the front of Compella's left shoulder. It is important to notice that I've kept his left arm at bay with my right hand.

I establish the Pyramid position by wrapping my left leg around the back of Compella's neck and bringing my right knee to the front of his left shoulder.

Triangle (push hand out)

In order to lock in the Triangle from the Pyramid control position, you must pull your foot out from underneath your opponent's arm. A lot of the time you can achieve this immediately after you transition into the Pyramid using the technique below. However, if your opponent shuts the triangle down by hugging onto your knee with his arm, then you will want to employ the technique that follows this one.

I've captured Einstein in the Pyramid position. It is important to notice that I'm pushing his left arm away from our bodies with my right hand.

I begin sliding my right knee underneath Einstein's left arm.

As I bring my right knee up toward my shoulder, my right foot comes out from underneath Einstein's left arm. Before he has a chance to counter, I wrap my right leg over his shoulder and elevate my left leg. To prevent Einstein from posturing up in this position, I maintain a tight over-hook on his right arm.

I place my right leg underneath my left knee.

To lock in the Triangle, I curl my left leg down to the mat, squeeze my knees together, and pull Einstein's head toward my chest with both hands.

Triangle (push hand up)

As I mentioned in the opening to the previous technique, sometimes gripping an opponent's wrist and forcing his arm to the outside doesn't work because he is latched tightly onto your knee. In such a scenario, I'll change my grip so that my palm is facing toward me. To break his hold and create the space needed to bring my knee in front of his shoulder, I'll drive his arm upward.

With Laurence trapped in the Pyramid position, immediately I think about catching him in a Triangle. My first instinct is to grab his wrist and shove it the outside, which would allow me to bring my right foot in front of his shoulder, but his left arm is locked tightly over my right knee. Instead of abandoning the Triangle, I decide to break his grip by pushing his arm upward. This will create the space I need to set up the Triangle.

Instead of grabbing Laurence's left wrist so that my palm is facing away from me, I grab it so that my palm is facing toward me. Immediately I use my grip to break his hold on my knee by driving his arm upward.

Keeping Laurence's left arm elevated with my right hand, I create enough space to sneak my right foot out from underneath his arm.

I wrap my right leg around the back of Laurence's head.

I hook my left knee over my right foot.

I lock in the Triangle by curling my left leg down to the mat, squeezing my knees together, and pulling Laurence's head toward my chest with both hands.

Tepee

Back in '96 a friend of mine named Scott Rodondo was having a hell of a time securing the Triangle choke because his legs were just too darn short. Not wanting to miss out on such an awesome submission, he changed the way he performed the Triangle. Instead of draping his leg across the back of his opponent's head, he'd wrap his arms around both of his knees and then squeeze. It looked crazy, and I actually discouraged him from using it. Convinced it wouldn't work, I put the technique out of my mind. Nearly ten years passed, and then one day a jiu-jitsu practitioner named Barret Yoshida came to my Academy. He showed me the move my friend had toyed with ten years prior. I gave it a try and loved it. My students loved it. In addition to being a useful tool for guys who had short legs, it also allowed you to catch opponents who were excellent at defending the normal Triangle. I asked Barret where he got the move, and he said he'd learned it from Erik Paulson. So we started calling it the Erik Paulson. After practice, you would hear guys saying, "Man, I got two Paulson's today." This went on for a while, and then one day Scott Rodondo showed up at 10th Planet. I just so happened to catch an opponent with the Paulson, and he instantly shouts out, "Dude, you just nailed the Tepee." At first I was like, "The Tepee? No dude, this is the Paulson." But then I thought about it, and I realized what must have happened. When Rodondo first showed me the move back in '96, he was training with me at Jean Jacques' academy. He left there shortly thereafter and went to train at Renato Magno's school. He must have showed some people there the move, and then it exploded and somehow reached Paulson's school. After all, both academies were located in the South Bay. Then Paulson showed it to Barret, and Barret brought it down to 10th Planet. Rodondo could have ragged on me for trying to discourage the move a decade prior, but instead he goes, "Dude, that move is better than the Triangle. It's just like doing a Lockdown with your legs, and then you wrap your arms around and squeeze. It's that simple." I agreed with him one hundred percent, and from that moment out I have been calling it the Tepee.

With Laurence trapped in the Pyramid position, immediately I think about catching him in a Triangle. My first instinct is to grab his wrist and shove it the outside, which would allow me to bring my right knee in front of his shoulder, but his left arm is locked tightly over my right knee. Instead of abandoning the Triangle, I decide to push his arm up to create the space I need to set up the Triangle.

Instead of grabbing Laurence's left wrist so that my palm is facing away from me, I grab it so that my palm is facing toward me. Immediately I break his hold on my knee by thrusting his arm upward.

Keeping Laurence's left arm elevated with my right hand, I create enough space to sneak my right foot out from underneath his arm.

Instead of draping my right leg across the back of Laurence's head, I hook my right foot under my left and squeeze my knees together.

As I begin to sit up, I spread my arms to wrap them around my legs.

I reach my arms all the way around my legs and form an S-grip with my hands just behind my knees. To lock in the submission, I straighten out my legs, squeeze my knees together, squeeze my arms around my knees, and elevate my hips. With my right knee being driven into left side of Laurence's neck, and Laurence's right shoulder being driven into the right side of his neck, the blood flow to his head is cut

Go-Go Plata to Loco Plata

The Go-Go Plata is another option you have from the Pyramid. It looks rather crazy because you're choking your opponent with your foot, but it's a wonderful move that works a high percentage of the time. However, sometimes your opponent will defend the Go-Go Plata by using his hand to push down on your foot. This frustrated me for some time, but then I came up with the Loco Plata, a technique that allows you to shut down your opponent's defense and still get the submission.

I have Laurence trapped in the Pyramid position. Anticipating that I will try to grab his left wrist and force his arm away from our bodies, he is hugging my right knee tightly.

Instead of grabbing his wrist and pushing it up, I bring my right forearm to the right side of Laurence's neck and hook my right wrist around my left leg. I refer to this movement as 'clearing the neck.'

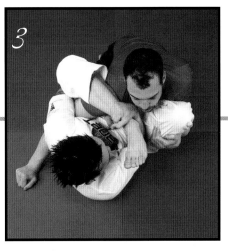

Using my right hook, I pull my left leg in front of Laurence's face.

I release my left over-hook and reach my left arm around the back of Laurence's head.

As I wrap my left arm around the back of Laurence's head, I use my right hand to shove my left foot into Laurence's neck.

Grabbing the top of my left foot with my left hand, I push on the heel of my left foot with my right hand, further digging my foot into Laurence's neck.

Pulling up on my left foot and driving my right palm into my left heel locks in the Go-Go Plata. If your opponent doesn't know the counter to this move, he will either tap or pass out.

In an attempt to avoid tapping, Laurence reaches up and peels my left foot away from his throat.

I grab Laurence's left wrist with my right hand.

Immediately I drive Laurence's left arm away from our bodies.

Lifting my right knee toward my shoulder, I place my right heel underneath my left heel. To lock in the Loco Plata, I pull up on my left foot and use my right heel to further drive my left foot into Laurence's neck.

Inverted Arm Bar

When you secure the Pyramid control position, a lot of opponents will grow anxious because they know you have several options at your disposal. In addition to latching onto your leg to avoid the Triangle, they might also try to pull their trapped arm free from your over-hook so they can posture up. In such a scenario, you have a small window of opportunity to submit your opponent with the Inverted Arm Bar. Timing is everything with this move. As your opponent is pulling his arm free, you have to clamp your over-hook down at just the right time. You want to catch his arm just above his elbow. If you clamp down too late or too soon, the chances are you won't be able to hyperextend your opponent's arm.

I have Laurence trapped in the Pyramid position. I am trying to force his left arm away from our bodies with my right hand, but his grip on my right knee is too tight to break.

As Laurence tries to pull his trapped arm free, I clear his neck with my right arm, hook my right wrist around my left leg, and then pull my left leg in front of his face.

I quickly clasp my hands together using a Gable Grip and hook my left foot underneath Laurence's chin. To lock in the Inverted Arm Bar, I extend my left leg, squeeze my left hook into Laurence's arm, and turn slightly to my right side. It is important to notice that my left arm is hooked just above Laurence's right elbow. If your arm is positioned much lower or higher, you won't be able to hyperextend your opponent's arm.

Kung Fu Move to Jiu-Claw

The Pyramid is a huge part of the Rubber Guard system because the Triangle is right there, waiting for you to take it. But if the Triangle isn't happening because you can't pull your leg up and wrap it around your opponent's neck, you still have a wonderful option—the Omaplata. All you have to do is clear your opponent's neck with your forearm, execute the Kung Fu Move, and go right into Jiu-Claw and the Omaplata.

I've got Compella in the Pyramid.

I release Compella's left wrist and move my right forearm to the right side of his head.

I hook my right wrist around my left leg.

Using my right hook, I pull my left leg down in front of Compella's face.

I release my left over-hook on Compella's right arm and latch onto my left knee. At the same time, I execute the Kung Fu Move by driving my left foot into Compella's face using the power of my leg and my right hand.

I continue to drive my left foot into Compella's face using the power of my left leg and right hand. I also push on my left knee with my left hand. My combined efforts pushes Compella away from me and allows me to pull my right leg out from underneath him.

Rotating my body in a clockwise direction, I obtain the Jiu-Claw position by wrapping my left arm around the back of Compella's legs and latching onto his right wrist with my right hand.

I bring my left foot underneath my right leg to secure the Jiu-Claw position.

The East Coast Croc

I see this scenario happen way to often—a guy works super hard to get his opponent's hand to the mat and reach New York, and then he lets his opponent free his arm. This doesn't have to occur. To secure your opponent's hand to the mat, all you have to do is hug your knee. It can be difficult to hold this position for a prolonged period of time, especially if your opponent is putting up a fight to free his arm, so it is crucial that you transition to Chill Dog as quickly as possible. This can be achieved by letting go of your ankle, clearing your arm over your opponent's head, and then digging your forearm into his neck. Sometimes this can be as easy as pie, but other times it can be quite difficult. If your opponent is keen to the Rubber Guard, he will do everything in his power to stop you from clearing his neck. In the case that he prevents you from obtaining your goal, you can utilize The East Coast Croc. As long as you can force your opponent's elbow across your chest using your leg, and then lock his shoulder, the Arm Bar will be yours for the taking.

I've got Laurence broken down into New York. My main goal from here is to get my right forearm to the right side of his neck, which will put me in Chill Dog. Laurence understands this, and he is doing everything in his power to stop me from clearing his neck. Instead of fighting him, I decide to execute the East Coast Croc.

I push off Laurence's left hip with my right foot. This gives me the momentum to swing my right leg away from our bodies in a clockwise direction.

As I swing my right leg back into my body, it collides with Laurence's left elbow and drives it over my stomach.

I pull my left leg down into the back of Laurence's head using my right hand, as well as pinch both of my knees together.

Pulling my left leg into the back of Laurence's head creates enough room for me to slide my right leg over his left shoulder.

Continuing to pinch my knees together, I place my left leg over my right foot. Notice how this locks Laurence's left shoulder and straightens his left arm.

I latch onto Laurence's left wrist with both hands. Making sure the thumb of his left hand is pointing upward, I lock in the submission by pulling his arm into my chest, curling my legs toward the mat, and elevating my hips.

Rescue Dog

When playing the Rubber Guard, most of the time you have a choice as to which side of your opponent's body you will attack. If you are like most jiu-jitsu practitioners, you'll probably get more comfortable attacking one side rather than the other. It's kind of like how things works with baseball players; they can hit from both sides, but they tend to lean to one side. This is all fine and dandy in the beginning—it's what allows you to get familiar with the techniques—but eventually you'll want to practice attacking the unfamiliar side as much as possible. There are several reasons for this. If your opponent learns that you can only attack one side, it doesn't take much for him to shut your entire game down. All he has to do is shut you down on one side and then you've got nowhere to go. The other reason is that if you get really good at attacking both sides, you can oftentimes catch your opponent off guard.

That's what we're going to do here. You're in New York trying to clear your opponent's neck to reach Chill Dog, but your opponent drives his head down and stops you from making the transition. He knows that he is in trouble because you've got his hand to the mat. He's doing everything in his power to protect that side of his body, which has taken his focus away from the other side of his body. In many cases, your opponent will inadvertently place his opposite hand on the mat. He's so worried about the arm you have trapped, he's not even considering what you can do with his other arm. With that whole side of his body open, you have a great opportunity to quickly secure Chill Dog on the opposite side and clear his neck. But the only way you'll have that option is if you work on improving your weak side at least a couple of times a week. To be the best jiu-jitsu player you can be, you must be able react off your opponent's movements and defense. If he gives you an opening, you have to be able to capitalize on that opening. I know it can be frustrating trying to improve your weak side—it can be like starting all over again—but trust me when I tell you that it will make your game a whole lot tighter in the long run.

I've got Laurence in New York.

I'm trying to bring my right arm over Laurence's head to reach Chill Dog, but he has stopped me from reaching my goal by defensively angling his head to his right side and driving his face into my chest.

Realizing Laurence has dropped his left hand to the mat, I quickly work to trap it there by dropping my left foot to his right hip, bringing my right leg up toward the back of his head, and circling my right arm towards the back of my right knee. From here I want to get my left forearm to the left side of his head before he can return his head to the center of my chest. This will allow me to bypass New York and head straight into Chill Dog.

I wrap my right arm around my right knee to secure Laurence's left hand to the mat. Because he had angled his head to his right side, I managed to get my left forearm to the left side of his head with little effort. I bypass New York and assume the Chill Dog control position by hooking my left arm over my right leg and digging my left forearm into his collarbone.

New York to Chill Dog

Once you trap your opponent's hand to the mat with New York, your next goal is to immediately transition into Chill Dog. It doesn't entail a complex series of movements; if you've got your left leg up, draped across the back of your opponent's head, all you have to do is move your right forearm from the left side of your opponent's neck to the right side of his neck. When grappling with an opponent who doesn't understand the Rubber Guard system, the transition can often be made without resistance. But when going up against someone familiar with the Rubber Guard, it can be a daunting task. Because he understands the path that you're traveling, he will go through great efforts to stop you from clearing his neck with your forearm. The trick to catching such opponents is speed and timing. If you can flow from Mission Control into New York, and then from New York into Chill Dog without missing a beat, you'll be one step ahead of him. While he is still focusing on how you trapped his hand to the mat, you'll be clearing his neck with your forearm. However, it is critical that you don't trade technique for speed. You have to remember to keep your opponent's arm trapped by hugging your knee. If you relax your grip and your opponent frees his arm, you will have to start over from ground zero.

I've got Laurence in New York. My next goal is to move my right elbow to the other side of his head, which will put me in Chill Dog.

Letting go of my left foot, I move my right arm towards the right side of Laurence's head. Notice how I am still trapping Laurence's right hand to the mat by hugging my left knee with my left arm. If I loosen my grip and Laurence pulls his arm free, I will have to start back at square one.

To create space, I drive my right forearm down across the right side of Laurence's head.

Having cleared Laurence's neck, I drive my right forearm down and to the right. This forces Laurence's head away from me and creates the space I need to assume the Chill Dog control position.

To secure Chill Dog, I hook my right wrist over my left leg, and then use that hook to pull my left leg down. To prevent Laurence from breaking free as I make my transition to Jiu-Claw, I will need to keep everything locked tight.

Arm Bar

When you reach Chill Dog, the first thing you should do is test the Invisible Collar Submission, which you learn about shortly. If you can't get the submission tight enough to force your opponent to tap, then your next goal should be to transition to the Jiu-Claw control position. It's nice when this transition comes easy, but most of the time you'll encounter some type of resistance. In this particular scenario, your opponent tries to get his head back to the center of your chest by breaking your grips with his free arm. You have a couple of different options when this occurs. You can fight him and try to maintain Chill Dog, or you can use his struggle to transition into an Arm Bar. I'll usually choose the latter because my opponent is offering me a way to end the fight.

Laurence knows he is in trouble now that I've got him in Chill Dog. In an effort to escape, he tries to break my grips by punching his left arm to the inside of my right arm. If he can straighten his arm out, it will be very difficult for me to continue to grip my left leg with my right hand.

Instead of fighting Laurence, I decide to use his positioning to transition into an Arm Bar. Immediately I push my right foot of his left hip. Using that momentum, I swing my leg out and up toward our heads.

As I swing my leg around to the right side of Laurence's head, his left arm gets shoved across my chest. I encounter very little resistance because Laurence was already driving his arm in this direction in an effort to break my grips.

Without hesitation, I let go of my left leg and grab Laurence's left wrist with both hands. As I do this, I coil my legs toward the mat and extend my hips upward.

Still curling my legs toward the mat and elevating my hips, I pull down on Laurence's wrist with both hands and hyperextend his arm.

Carni

A lot of opponents will get desperate or anxious when you have them in Chill Dog. In addition to latching onto your knee to prevent you from transitioning into Jiu-Claw, they will sometimes push down on your trapped leg and step over it in an effort to escape. When this happens, it puts you in a Chill Dog/ half guard position and gives you a couple of different options. You can abandon Chill Dog and secure the Lockdown, in which case you would work from half guard, or you can utilize your current positioning and transition to the Omaplata. I usually choose the latter because my opponent just put himself into a position where he can't stop me from locking his shoulder. Once I lock his shoulder, all I have to do to force him to tap is grab his wrist and jack his arm. However, when going for this move your opponent still has an out. The move requires that you trap your opponent's leg to the mat using your leg. If he is flexible, he can pull his leg out from underneath your leg by doing the splits. Then he can execute a roll and escape the submission. This happens, but it doesn't happen too often. If you execute the move quickly, usually you can force your opponent to tap before he has a chance to figure out how to untangle himself. The reason I call this technique the Carni is because even though your opponent thinks he is defeating your Rubber Guard by forcing half guard, it ain't over until the fat lady sings. I would have called it something else, but I couldn't think of a singer fatter than Carni Wilson.

I've got Laurence in Chill Dog.

Laurence realizes he is in trouble. In an attempt to escape Chill Dog, he forces my right leg down to the mat with his left hand, and then he steps his left foot over my leg. His current goal is to pass my guard and then free his trapped arm.

As Laurence steps over my leg, I maintain the Chill Dog position. It is important not to abandon the position at the first sign of trouble. If you maintain your composure, a solution will usually present itself.

Using my right hand, I start pulling my left leg down in front of Laurence's face. I also straighten my right leg over Laurence's left leg. This traps his leg to the mat and prevents him from escaping the submission by executing a forward roll.

I switch the position of my right hand; instead of hooking under my left foot, I grab the top of my foot. Once I've got a good hold, I execute the Kung Fu Move by pushing Laurence's head away using both my left foot and right hand.

I continue to drive Laurence's head away from me using my left foot and right hand. It is important to notice that I am still hugging my left knee. It is also important to notice that I'm keeping my right leg straight, pinning Laurence's left leg to the mat. Both of these actions are crucial. If I were to let go of my knee, Laurence would have an opportunity to free his right arm. If I weren't pinning his left leg to the mat, he could escape the submission by executing a forward roll.

Now that my left foot is dug all the way in front of Laurence's face, I remove my left hand from my knee and replace it with my right. Applying downward pressure with my right hand helps keep Laurence's arm trapped. At the same time, I grab his right wrist with my left hand. It is important to notice that I'm gripping with my palm pointing up.

Once I have my left grip secure, I latch onto Laurence's wrist with my right hand as well. To apply the submission, I simply push his arm upward.

Crowbar

As I have already mentioned, an opponent familiar with the Rubber Guard system will know your intentions the moment you reach Chill Dog. He'll keep your leg trapped tightly in his armpit to stop you from transitioning to the Jiu-Claw control position. Most of the time you will be able to free your leg as long as you're patient, but sometimes your opponent won't let you budge. In such a scenario, you can utilize the Crowbar. It requires that you let go of your knee, which is far from optimal because it gives your opponent a chance to pull his trapped arm free. To prevent this from happening, you must be quick to punch your hand underneath your opponent's neck and straighten out your arm. This creates enough space to pull your trapped leg out from underneath your opponent and complete your transition to Jiu-Claw. It's a powerful move when done with speed and proper technique.

I've got Laurence in Chill Dog. He knows that I am only one step away from transitioning into the Jiu-Claw control position. In an attempt to stop me from making that transition, he latches onto my right leg and traps it in his armpit.

I circle my left arm around to the front of my knee. From here I want to slide my left arm down the right side of Laurence's face and then across his throat. It is important that you execute this step quickly because now that you have let go of your knee, your opponent has a window of opportunity to pull his right arm free. The faster you jam your forearm across your opponent's throat, the smoother your transition to Jiu-Claw will be.

With my left thumb pointing toward the mat, I punch my left hand across Laurence's neck.

Coming up onto my right elbow, I create the space needed to transition into the Jiu-Claw position by straightening my left arm. As I drive Laurence back, I follow him up.

As I come up with Laurence, I wrap my left arm around his back for control and slide my right leg out from underneath his body. Immediately I hook my left foot underneath my right leg. This is the riskiest part of the transition. If you don't control your opponent with your left arm, he will be able to roll out. If you don't lock your legs tightly, your opponent will be able to pull his arm free. It is imperative that you act quickly and maintain control of your opponent.

I transition into the Jiu-Claw position by sitting back, wrapping my left arm around the back of Laurence's legs, and controlling his right wrist with my right hand. To learn about your options from here, see the Jiu-Claw series.

Mad Dog Control

Utilizing Mad Dog Control is another way that you can make the transition from Chill Dog to Jiu-Claw when your opponent is hugging your leg. Instead of waiting for your opponent to release your leg, you assume the Mad Dog Control position and force your leg out inch by inch. Although you might only get an inch every thirty seconds, it's safer than the utilizing the Crowbar because your opponent won't have that blatant window of opportunity to escape. It offers the ultimate control, especially if you are wearing gi pants, knee sleeves, or Tubigrip. As long as you are patient, you'll eventually get your leg up and reach Jiu-Claw.

I've got Laurence in Chill Dog.

I pull my left leg down with both hands. Instantly I realize that Laurence's defenses are strong, that I won't be able to create enough space with the Kung Fu Move to free my right leg. I decide to use Mad Dog Control instead.

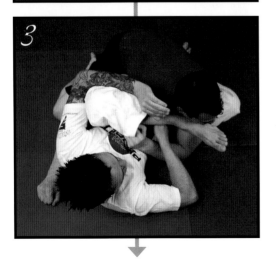

Still hugging my left knee with my left arm, I release my right hook on my left leg.

I clasp my hands together using a Gable Grip and pull my left knee toward my chest, locking Laurence to my body. From here, I can take my time and slowly transition into the Jiu-Claw control position.

Continuing to pull down on my left knee, I turn onto my right side. This forces Laurence's right shoulder down to the mat and creates enough space for me to pull my right leg out from underneath his body.

As I draw my right leg out from underneath Laurence's body, I grab his right wrist with my right hand. To stop him from freeing his arm, I hook my left foot underneath my right knee.

Still controlling Laurence's right wrist with my right hand, I hook my left arm around the back of his legs. This puts me in the Jiu-Claw position. To discover your options from here, visit the Jiu-Claw section.

Chill Dog to Invisible Collar

Opponents familiar with the Rubber Guard System will usually latch onto your leg when you're in Chill Dog, hindering you from pulling your leg all the way out and making the transition to Jiu-Claw and the Omaplata. The Invisible Collar is another way of dealing with this dilemma. While it might be difficult to pull your leg out from underneath your opponent's arm, it's usually possible to bring your leg over his arm to a certain degree. If you can bring it over enough to hook your feet together, the Invisible Collar submission is right there. I call it the Invisible Collar because it resembles a traditional gi choke. The only difference is instead of latching onto your opponent's collar, you're latching onto your ankle. I wouldn't go so far as to call it a high percentage submission, but it certainly puts your opponent in a great deal of pain. This is particularly true with the big guys because their bulk will lock everything tight. Some guys will tap under the pressure, and some guys won't—it all depends upon how tight the submission is locked and your opponent's tolerance to pain.

I've got Laurence in Chill Dog. Before I make my transition into Jiu-Claw, I will see if I can finish him with the Invisible Collar.

Pushing my right foot off Laurence's hip, I swing my right leg up and over my left foot. Then I hook my feet and squeeze everything nice and tight. I'm curling both arms in, applying downward pressure with my legs, and crunching my abs as if I were trying to sit up. These little nuances help drive my right forearm into Laurence's collarbone and neck, hopefully causing him enough pain to tap.

Invisible Collar Variation

The Invisible Collar is one of those rare moves that works better on the larger opponents. The bulkier the guy is, the more pressure you can apply to his neck. On occasion you can catch a smaller guy with the Invisible Collar, but it's really hard to cause them much pain with the submission. This bothered me for some time, and then I came up with an Invisible Collar variation specifically designed to catch the smaller opponents. It allows you to lock everything so tight that you can't even apply it on the big guys. As soon as I started doing this, my success rate with the Invisible Collar shot up twenty percent.

I've got Compella in the Invisible Collar, but I can't get it tight enough to force him to tap. Instead of abandoning the submission, I decide to utilize the Invisible Collar Variation.

I grab the top of my right foot with my left hand. It is important to notice that my left arm is still wrapped around my knee to keep Laurence's hand trapped to the mat.

With the standard Invisible Collar I was gripping my left leg with my right hand. Instead of holding onto that grip, I reach my right hand up and grip my right ankle.

Now that my hold is super tight, I pull down with both arms, flex my abs as if I were doing a sit up, and drive my elbow into Compella's collarbone. It is important to notice that I'm not perfectly squared up with Compella; my lower body is hanging off to my right side. This allows me to apply the maximum amount of pressure.

Go-Go Plata to Loco Plata

If you're in a competition and your opponent is all hopped up off adrenaline, a lot of times he won't tap to the pain caused by the Invisible Collar submission. In such a scenario, you can execute the Kung Fu Move and transition into Jiu-Claw or you can apply the Go-Go Plata and try to finish him. The latter is a tricky move that requires a certain degree of flexibility, but it can be extremely effective in the right hands. Once you have the submission locked in, your opponent's main defense will be to grab your foot to prevent you from choking him with it. That's when the Loco Plata comes into play.

I've got Laurence in the Invisible Collar. I've locked it down as tight as I can and he still isn't tapping, so I decide to go for the Go-Go Plata.

Unhooking my feet, I use my right hand to pull my left leg down in front of Laurence's face.

I drive my left foot underneath Laurence's chin with my right hand and reach around the back of his head with my left hand.

I grab onto the top of my left foot with my left hand and use my right palm to drive my foot into his neck. This is the Go-Go Plata submission, from which many opponents will tap.

Laurence knows how to defend against the Go-Go Plata. He grabs my foot with his left hand and peels it away from his neck, alleviating the pressure.

In order to salvage the submission, I transition to the Loco Plata. I do this by grabbing Laurence's left wrist with my right hand and then forcing his defending arm away from our bodies. It is important to notice that I've gripped Laurence's wrist with my palm facing up.

Still holding Laurence's arm out to the side, I bring my right foot underneath his arm. To lock in the Loco Plata, I drive my right heel up into my left heel. Having removed Laurence's only line of defense from the picture, his only option is to tap.

Invisible Crocodile

Many opponents will attempt to defend the Invisible Collar submission by pushing your elbow away from their neck. Although this can make the Invisible Collar hard to execute, it allows you to bring the Invisible Crocodile into play.

I've got Laurence in the Invisible Collar.

Laurence defends by pushing my right elbow away from his neck and collarbone. Instead of fighting, I release my right grip on my left leg and unhook my feet. Because my right arm is no longer anchored, it allows Laurence to shove my elbow away from his neck. To ensure that he doesn't posture up, I continue to trap his arm to the mat by hugging my left knee.

As Laurence pushes my elbow away from his neck, his elbow moves closer to the center of my chest. I help guide his elbow along using my right knee. It is important to keep everything as tight as possible while making this transition.

I lock Laurence's left shoulder with my right leg, grab his wrist with both hands, and elevate my hips.

To finish the submission, I squeeze my knees together, elevate my hips, apply downward pressure with my legs, and pull Laurence's arm to my chest. It is important to notice that I've grabbed Laurence's wrist in such a way that his thumb is pointed upward. It is important that you remember to do this or the submission won't work.

Far Side Arm Bar

In the previous technique I showed you how to catch an opponent in an Arm Bar when he attempts to alleviate the pressure you've put on his neck with the Invisible Collar. Although a lot of opponents will behave in such a manner, some will simply endure the pain. This is especially true in competition where adrenaline runs high. In such a scenario, a good option is to transition from the Invisible Collar to the Far Side Arm Bar.

I've got Laurence in the Invisible Collar, but he is not tapping. I decide to transition to the Far Side Arm Bar.

Releasing my hold on my left knee, I grab the top of my right foot with my left hand.

I pull my right foot in front of Laurence's face.

Releasing the grips I have on my leg and foot, I grab Laurence's left wrist with both hands.

Driving my right leg up into Laurence's face, I elevate my hips and straighten his arm on my chest. It is important to grab your opponent's wrist with both hands and position his arm so that his thumb is pointing upward.

I wrap the crook of my right leg around the right side of Laurence's head. To lock in the Far Side Arm Bar, I apply downward pressure with my legs, elevate my hips, and pull Laurence's arm to my chest using both hands.

Swim Move

I showed this move in my last book, but I really didn't use it that much. I just couldn't see the sense in going through all that work to trap my opponent's hand to the mat, and then turn around and scoop his hand off the mat to force his arm across my chest. I put the technique on the back burner, but then one of my students up in San Francisco told me how much success he was having with the technique. I decided to go back to it, and I began to see it in a different light. It's a beautiful move because from the Invisible Collar there is very little your opponent can do to prevent you from pushing his arm across your chest. The key is to get a really deep hook on your opponent's arm. When you spin and reach for your opponent's hip, that hook is what keeps everything together. Hooking your opponent's wrist won't work; you've got to have the crook of your arm wrapped around the crook of your opponent's arm to be successful. Learn how to manage that, and you will have a good chance of transitioning to the Spider Web position.

I've got Laurence in the Invisible Collar.

Letting go of my left knee, I push Laurence's right elbow across my body using my left hand.

Once I push Laurence's right arm toward the center of my chest, I turn over onto my right side and slide my left arm over his right arm, securing a deep hook. It is important that you don't just drape your arm over your opponent's arm, but rather reach your left hand toward your right hip to get your hook sunk really deep. Ideally, you want the crook of your arm wrapped around the crook of your opponent's arm.

I unhook my feet and release my right grip on my left leg. Then in one motion I sprawl my right arm out on the mat above me and roll over toward my stomach. As I do this, I drive my left leg down into the back of Laurence's head and drive my right leg up into his hips. It is important to note that if you don't keep your hook on your opponent's arm tight during the roll, you may lose the submission and your position.

As I continue to roll, I drive my left knee down into the mat. It is important to notice how I am rolling over my left shoulder and keeping my head to my right.

As I roll over onto my back, I force Laurence to complete his roll by scissoring my legs. My left leg is driving into the back of Laurence's head, and my right leg is driving into his midsection. At the same time, I hook my right arm around the back of Laurence's right leg to prevent a scramble as I transition into the Spider Web position.

Continuing to scissor my legs, Laurence completes his roll and comes down onto his back. Notice that my left arm is still hooked around his right arm, and my right arm is still hooked around his right leg.

As Laurence comes all the way down onto his back, I place my left leg over his head and cross my feet underneath his left shoulder. I maintain control of his right leg with my right arm to prevent a scramble, and I keep my left arm hooked deep around his right arm. To discover your options from here, visit the Spider Web section.

Kung Fu Move to Jiu-Claw

As you probably realize by now, you will not be able to submit every opponent with the Invisible Collar. If your opponent has a high tolerance for pain, he might be able to endure the abuse for quite a while. You could potentially keep him there forever, try to wear him down over time, but at some point your legs will get tired. If you come to the conclusion that your opponent won't tap, transitioning to the Jiu-Claw is a great option. With your opponent focusing on trying to survive the Invisible Collar rather than trapping your leg, you can usually execute the Kung Fu Move and reach Jiu-Claw without much resistance. Once you get to Jiu-Claw, it is important that you secure your opponent's wrist and wrap your arm around the back of his legs. Failure to do either will give your opponent an opportunity to escape and achieve side control.

I've got Laurence in the Invisible Collar. Although I can't apply enough pressure to force him to tap, I can tell the submission is distracting him. I decide to use the distraction to execute the Kung Fu Move and transition into the Jiu-Claw position.

Unhooking my feet, I pull my left foot in front of Laurence's face using my right hand. As I do this, I continue to hug my left knee to keep his right hand pinned to the mat.

Having brought my left foot in front of Laurence's face, I switch my grip by placing my right hand on the top of my left foot.

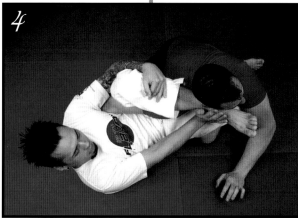

I execute the Kung Fu Move by driving my foot into Laurence's face using the power of my leg and my right hand. Notice that I'm still hugging my left knee to keep his right hand pinned to the mat.

Continuing to drive my left foot into Laurence's face, I spin my body in a clockwise direction. This allows me to pull my right leg out from underneath Laurence's body. To ensure that he can't pull his right arm free, I latch onto his wrist with my right hand.

I reach my left hand behind Laurence's legs to gain control of the lower half of his body, and I hook my left foot underneath my right leg to lock his shoulder. To discover your options from here, visit the Jiu-Claw section.

Omaplata

When you make it to the Jiu-Claw control position, you can head right into the Omaplata. However, it's not the quickest submission out there. It requires that you sit up and flare your legs out wide. If your opponent is an experienced jiu-jitsu practitioner, he will have some time to realize your intentions and defend the submission by rolling over onto his shoulder. This shouldn't detour you from attempting the Omaplata; it should simply make you anticipate your opponent's defense. If you're paying attention when he attempts to roll out of the submission, you can transition right into the DA, which you will learn about shortly. Becoming a master at countering your opponent's defense is key to developing a dangerous game.

I have Compella trapped in the Jiu-Claw position. Although my mindset is on attacking, I'm prepared to counter if he should attempt an escape.

Because Compella doesn't attempt to escape, I immediately coil my left leg under my right, sit up, and reach my left arm over his back to prevent him from rolling over onto his right shoulder. Notice how I'm still controlling Compella's right wrist with my right hand. It is very important that you do this until you flare your legs out and secure the submission.

As I continue to sit up, I flare my right leg back, reach my left around Compella's back, slide my right arm underneath his head, and then clasp my hands together using an S-grip beneath his chin. To lock in the Omaplata, I lean forward, use my arms to pull my hips up, and drive my left knee down into Compella's trapped arm. This puts a tremendous amount of pressure on his shoulder and forces him to tap.

The Ice Pick

A lot of times when you get an opponent in the Jiu-Claw position, he will try to posture up to free his trapped arm. If you have your legs positioned correctly, this won't be much of an issue. Every time he comes up, you drive him back down with your legs. I call this technique the Ice Pick, and when you put force behind it, you will not only drive your opponent's face into the mat, but you will also set yourself up for the Omaplata. Going for the Omaplata off the Ice Pick will increase your success rate with the submission significantly, but you still won't get it all of the time. If your opponent is full of energy and ready to fight, he will do everything in his power to defend against the submission. This too won't be much of an issue as long as you are ready to counter his defense with another technique such as the DA. The Omaplata is a great submission, but when heading into it, you must always anticipate that your opponent will attempt to escape, as well as understand how you can use his escape attempt to your advantage.

I've got Laurence in the Jiu-Claw position.

Laurence attempts to escape by posturing up. Notice how I maintain control of his right wrist and keep my left arm wrapped around the back of his legs. If you do not maintain this control, you will lose the submission and perhaps the dominant positioning you worked so hard to achieve.

To break Laurence's posture, I squeeze my knees together and straighten out my legs. It is similar to stretching your opponent out with the Lockdown, except here you have your opponent's arm trapped rather than his leg.

Pushing in on Laurence's elbow with my right leg, I drive my left leg down into his shoulder. Laurence has no choice but to face plant into the mat.

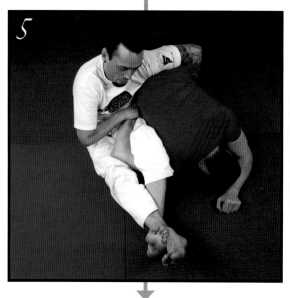

Now that Laurence's posture is completely broken, I use the momentum from the Ice Pick to sit up. Immediately I reach my left arm over his back to prevent him from rolling over his shoulder. Notice that I still have control of his right wrist.

As I sit all the way up, I flare my right leg back behind me. With my forward pressure now trapping Laurence's right arm between my thigh and hip, I can let go of his wrist.

I slide my right hand over Laurence's right shoulder and then reach underneath his head.

I clasp my hands together using an S-grip underneath Laurence's chin. To lock in the Omaplata submission, I lean forward, use my arms to pull my hips up, and apply downward pressure on Laurence's right shoulder with my left knee.

Inverted Arm Bar

The Omaplata is just a few steps away when you reach Jiu-Claw, but sometimes your opponent's arm is positioned in such a way that it prevents you from sitting up and applying the shoulder lock. Other times your opponent may free his arm after you Ice Pick him down. There is no reason to abandon the Jiu-Claw position in either situation because you can go right to the Inverted Arm Bar.

I've got Laurence in the Jiu-Claw position.

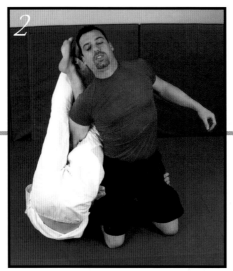

Laurence attempts to escape by posturing up. Notice how I maintain control of his right wrist and keep my left arm wrapped around the back of his legs. If you do not maintain this control, you will lose the submission and perhaps the dominant positioning you worked so hard to achieve.

Pushing in on Laurence's elbow with my right leg, I drive my left leg down into his shoulder. Laurence has no choice but to face plant into the mat.

To lock Laurence's shoulder, I continue to squeeze my knees together and straighten out my legs.

To apply the Inverted Arm Bar, I sit up and straighten Laurence's arm out with my right hand. As I do this, I keep my knees pinched together and my legs straight. All I'm doing here is maintaining downward pressure with my legs and using my knee as a fulcrum to hyperextend his arm.

Arm Bar

This is another way to set up the Inverted Arm Bar. The chance that you will get the submission is slim, but in this case that's not your intentions. Your only reason for applying the Inverted Arm Bar is to force your opponent into a forward roll. When he does this, he lands right in the Spider Web position, allowing you to submit him with an Arm Bar. I got this move from some jiu-jitsu player who had learned it from BJ Penn.

I've got Laurence in the Jiu-Claw position.

Laurence attempts to escape by posturing up. Notice how I maintain control of his right wrist and keep my left arm wrapped around the back of his legs.

I break Laurence's posture by squeezing my knees together and driving my left leg down into his right shoulder.

The moment I break Laurence's posture, I lift my left leg up so that I can shove my right foot underneath his armpit.

Wedging my right foot underneath Laurence's armpit, I curl my left leg toward the mat.

I pull Laurence's right arm away from his body with my right hand.

Grabbing Laurence's right wrist with both hands, I drive his arm upwards. Laurence now has two options; he can either tap to the Inverted Arm Bar or escape the submission by executing a forward roll.

As Laurence rolls forward, I remove my left leg from his shoulder and hook my left foot under his hip. This not only allows me to control his roll with my foot, but it also sets me up for the Arm Bar.

Still latching onto Laurence's arm with both hands, I guide him over to his back using my legs. It is important to notice the positioning of my left leg. Although I'm using it to help Laurence along, I've kept it close to his head, which is where I want to place it the moment he comes down to his back. If you don't get your leg over your opponent's head the moment he comes down, you will most likely lose the submission.

As Laurence rolls over to his back, I drive my right leg over his chest and curl my left leg over his face. To lock in the Arm Bar, I apply downward pressure with my legs to keep Laurence from posturing up, pinch my knees together, elevate my hips, and pull his arm to my chest with both hands.

Triangle

Most of the time when an opponent postures up in the Jiu-Claw position, I will Ice Pick him back down and immediately transition into one of the Jiu-Claw options. I catch a lot of opponents this way, but sometimes I go up against a guy who has really sharp defense. To switch things up, I'll go for the Triangle when he postures up. If the submission doesn't work because I can't get his arm across my body, then I will transition into the Omaplata. If the Omaplata doesn't work because he postures up and turns into me, than I will go back to the Triangle. They work very well with one another, and you can go back and forth between them until you land one. The trick to catching an opponent with sharp defense is to throw everything at him but the kitchen sink.

I've got Laurence in the Jiu-Claw position.

As Laurence postures up, I decide to go for the Triangle. Maintaining control of his right wrist with my right hand, I unhook my feet but keep my left leg curled tightly over his right shoulder so I can continue to apply downward pressure.

Pulling Laurence's right arm across my body, I swing my right leg in a counter-clockwise direction and wrap it around the back of his head.

I pull Laurence down by curling my right leg into the back of his head. Then I hook the crook of my left leg over my right foot.

To lock in the Triangle, I squeeze my knees together, flex my toes, and pull Laurence's head toward my chest with both hands.

FM Ankle Lock (near leg)

Many opponents will expect you to attempt the Omaplata when you get them into the Jiu-Claw position. If they prepare their defense ahead of time, it can sometimes be a difficult submission to pull off. A good approach against such opponents is to abandon the Omaplata for another submission. I'll usually go to the Triangle, but on occasion I will also attack my opponent's ankles. This technique works particularly well on opponents who put their entire focus into defending their upper body. By the time they realize you're attacking their legs, it's too late. Frank Mir made this option off the Jiu-Claw very popular by using it to submit Tank Abbott a few years ago.

I've got Laurence in the Jiu-Claw position.

Laurence attempts to escape by posturing up. Notice how I maintain control of his right wrist, as well as keep my left arm wrapped around the back of his legs. If you do not maintain this control, you will lose the submission and perhaps the dominant positioning you worked so hard to achieve.

I break Laurence's posture by squeezing my knees together and driving my left leg down into his right shoulder.

The moment I break Laurence down, I scoop my left elbow underneath his right leg and grip the top of his foot.

Releasing my grip on Laurence's wrist, I slide my right arm over his leg and latch onto my left wrist. It is important to notice that I'm gripping with my right palm facing up.

As I push Laurence's foot up with my left hand, I drive my right elbow towards the mat. This torques his ankle in a clockwise direction and forces him to tap.

FM Ankle Lock (far leg)

If your opponent is real close to you, sometimes it can be difficult to slip your arm underneath his near leg and apply the previous submission. In such cases, attacking his far ankle is a better option.

I've got Laurence in the Jiu-Claw position.

Laurence attempts to escape by posturing up. Notice how I maintain control of his right wrist, as well as keep my left arm wrapped around the back of his legs.

I break Laurence's posture by squeezing my knees together and driving my left leg down into his right shoulder.

Releasing my grip on Laurence's wrist, I reach over and grab the top of his left foot with my right hand. It is important to notice that my right hand is hooked underneath Laurence's foot.

Pulling Laurence's left foot toward my chest, I wrap my left arm around his left leg and latch onto my right wrist.

To lock in the submission, I push up with my right hand and pull my left arm down. This torques Laurence's ankle and forces him to tap.

DA

The Omaplata doesn't have a highest success rate from the Jiu-Claw position. In my opinion, there are usually better options at your disposal. I say 'usually' because most of those options are based upon your opponent's reactions. If he just lies there, the Omaplata is probably your best bet, but most of the time your opponent will give his best effort to escape the Jiu-Claw position. He can achieve this by rolling in a couple of different directions, and you have to learn how to capitalize on his various escape options. If you just let your opponent roll fast in any direction that he wants, he will get the escape. But if you learn how to control his roll, it can set you up for a sweep that will land you on top. This is what the DA is all about. At first the technique might land you in your opponent's guard because you're not used to controlling the roll, but eventually you'll learn how to turn that scramble into a move.

I've got Laurence in the Jiu-Claw position.

Laurence attempts to escape by posturing up. Notice how I maintain control of his right wrist, as well as keep my left arm wrapped around the back of his legs.

I break Laurence's posture by squeezing my knees together and driving my left leg down into his right shoulder.

I continue to squeeze my knees together and straighten out my legs. As Laurence begins to roll over onto his right shoulder, I lean toward my right side and pull him on top of me with my left hand. It is important to notice that I'm still controlling his right wrist with my right hand.

As Laurence heads further into his roll, I sit up with him. Notice how I am controlling his roll with my left hand. This is very important. If you do not control the speed of your opponent's roll, your opponent may be able to quickly scramble and escape.

Unhooking my feet and flaring my right leg back, I continue to control Laurence's roll by sitting up and pushing into his body.

As Laurence nears the end of his roll, I bring my left elbow in tight to my body and push his legs out of the way with my right hand.

To assume the Twister Side Control position, I slide my left elbow across Laurence's body.

The Un-Winder

The DA is a wonderful move because it counters the most common escape from the Jiu-Claw position, which is the roll. However, another legitimate escape is the duck-under. This is where your opponent ducks underneath your legs and uses his momentum to throw you over, which will place him on top. The key to countering the duck-under is to see it coming and then relax. If you maintain a strong Lockdown on your opponent's arm and stay tensed up, your opponent will have no problem getting to the top position, but if you go limp the second you see the duck-under coming, then it becomes much harder for your opponent to throw you. This allows you to step over the top of him and obtain side control.

I've got Laurence in the Jiu-Claw position.

Laurence attempts to escape by posturing up. Notice how I maintain control of his right wrist, as well as keep my left arm wrapped around the back of his legs.

I break Laurence's posture by squeezing my knees together and driving my left leg down into his right shoulder.

As I break Laurence down, he attempts the duck-under escape by rolling over onto his left shoulder.

Laurence continues to roll over onto his back. If I were to keep my body stiff, Laurence would be able to throw my body to his right with his roll. To keep that from happening, I let my body go limp. Notice how I simply ride my weight on top of him.

I flare my legs out wide as I land on Laurence's right side. This prevents him from being able to use the momentum of his roll to create separation between our bodies. If you let your opponent get that separation, he will most likely escape.

Sliding my left elbow over to Laurence's right side lands me in Twister Side Control.

The Snitch

This technique is very similar to the DA because your opponent is executing a forward roll in an attempt to escape the Jiu-Claw control position. I'll choose this technique over the DA when I feel my opponent rolling into me rather than away from me. Instead of bringing my right arm in and securing Twister Side Control immediately after the roll, as I do in the DA, I will continue to control my opponent's legs and move around to the other side of his body to establish standard side control.

I've got Laurence in the Jiu-Claw position.

Laurence attempts to escape by posturing up. Notice how I maintain control of his right wrist, as well as keep my left arm wrapped around the back of his legs.

I break Laurence's posture by squeezing my knees together and driving my left leg down into his right shoulder.

I continue to squeeze my knees together and straighten out my legs. As Laurence begins to roll over onto his right shoulder, I lean toward my right side and pull him on top of me with my left hand. It is important to notice that I'm still controlling his right wrist with my right hand.

As Laurence heads further into his roll, I sit up with him. Notice how I am controlling his roll with my left hand. This is very important. If you do not control the speed of your opponent's roll, your opponent may be able to quickly scramble and escape.

Instead of allowing Laurence to roll like I did in the DA, I maintain control of his legs with my left arm and start walking around his legs to assume side control on his left side.

I drop my base down low and distribute my weight over Laurence's legs. If you do not keep your weight distributed over your opponent, you will lose control of the scramble.

As I come around to Laurence's left side, I post my right leg out to the side and reach my right hand around his left shoulder.

Walking all the way around to Laurence's left side, I dig my right knee underneath his shoulder and my left knee underneath his hip. To keep his shoulders pinned to the mat, I assume head and arm control by clasping my hands together underneath his right shoulder using a Gable Grip.

MASTERING THE RUBBER GUARD

The Drowning Jiu

Sometimes when you Ice Pick your opponent to the mat from the Jiu-Claw position, you lose control of his arm. This takes away the majority of leverage you had on his shoulder, and it won't be long until he pulls his arm free from between your legs. To keep your opponent from accomplishing this and achieving a top position, you'll have a small window of opportunity to make the transition to Spider Web. It is not a technique you should use outright—maintaining control of your opponent's arm is much better—but it works great as a fail-safe.

I've got Laurence in the Jiu-Claw position.

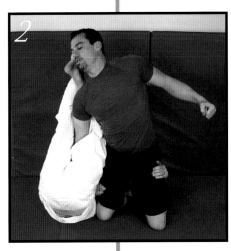

Laurence attempts to escape by posturing up. Notice how I maintain control of his right wrist, as well as keep my left arm wrapped around the back of his legs.

I break Laurence's posture by squeezing my knees together and driving my left leg down into his right shoulder.

Laurence frees his right arm from my grasp and loops it around my right leg.

I quickly reach my left hand over Laurence's back, maneuver my right leg to the back of Laurence's head, post on my right elbow, and sit up.

Continuing to sit up, I pull my left leg out from underneath my right leg and place it over Laurence's back. At the same time, I slide my left arm underneath Laurence's right arm, establishing a deep hook. This last step is very important. If you hook your arm around your opponent's wrist rather than the cook of his arm, you will lose control of his arm while making your transition.

To secure my left hook on Laurence's arm, I grab my right hip with my left hand. Then I rotate up to my knees, driving my right knee down to the mat and my left instep into the back of Laurence's neck.

MASTERING THE RUBBER GUARD

Still driving my left instep into the back of Laurence's neck, I slide my right leg underneath his body. This is important because I will use my right leg to help force Laurence into a forward roll.

As I roll onto my left shoulder, I drive Laurence's head underneath his body with my left instep, and pull his upper body over his head with my right leg. I'm simply scissoring my legs to get him to go where I want. The moment Laurence starts going over, I quickly gain control of his right leg by grabbing his ankle with my right hand.

As Laurence rolls all the way over to his back, I wrap my right arm all the way around his right leg. This is a crucial step because it helps prevent Laurence from scrambling.

To trap Laurence in the Spider Web position, I place my left leg over the top of his head and hook my feet together underneath his left shoulder. To learn about your options from here, visit the Spider Web section.

Troubleshooting the Rubber Guard

Dealing with the Stack

A lot of jiu-jitsu practitioners ask me how to stop an opponent from stacking them when in the Rubber Guard. I tell them all the same thing—if an opponent has a really good stack, there is always the chance that he will shut down your Rubber Guard game. But that is all right because you still have some options. You can abandon Mission Control and go right into full guard. You can put your feet on your opponent's hips and elevate him over. You can get in your butterfly hooks and capitalize on his lack of balance by working your sweeps. If you can't get him over with a sweep because he posts his arm, it allows you to get your knee in front of his shoulder and start working your Rubber Guard techniques again. And if your opponent tries to stack you when you get to Chill Dog, you can use the stack against him by transitioning right into the Jiu-Claw Every time an opponent stands up to stack you, he is giving up his balance. It opens up a few options.

The trick to countering the stack is getting good at transitioning back and forth between the various guard positions. As your opponent drives his head and weight downward, you must be proficient at switching between the Rubber Guard and full guard; Rubber Guard and butterfly guard; butterfly guard back to the Rubber Guard. When your opponent feels you make one of these transitions from Mission Control, instinctively he will drop his weight back down to avoid a sweep.

The stack is something you have to learn how to deal with in every type of guard, not just the Rubber Guard. I hate it when people come up to me and say that they heard the stack can nullify the Rubber Guard. Dude, of course it can. The stack can nullify all guards. I mean, you don't have any of your weight backing up your techniques because you're lying on your friggen back. But the way to minimize the effectiveness of the stack is to learn how to move from one guard position to the next based upon your opponent's movements. This simply takes a lot of time on the mats.

Defending the Slam

If a guy is good at picking up his opponents and then slamming them down to the mat, it doesn't matter if you're using the Rubber Guard or the regular closed guard. A wrestler who has mastered the slam is going to pick you up either way. The trick to avoiding the slam is to sense it coming. The moment you feel your body start to come up, you have to hook your arm around the back of your opponent's knee. This will prevent your opponent from getting any height with your body, and eventually he will come back down. But if you react slowly, sometimes your arm will end up near your opponent's crotch and he will get enough height to dish out some pain. To avoid such damage, you must always anticipate the slam. I don't care what you are working for in Mission Control or Crack Head Control—you must expect that your opponent will try and slam you at any moment.

To help drill this into my student's heads at 10th Planet, the second they get picked up they have to release their hold on their opponent. I don't care if they have a Triangle locked in tight—if they get picked up, they just lost. They have to start all over with breaking their opponent down in their full guard. It forces them to remember to wrap an arm around their opponent's leg the moment they start getting hefted off the mat. The reason I'm so harsh with this is because of what can happen out on the street. If an adversary picks you up and you try to hold onto a submission, you could very easily die upon impact. Getting slammed onto concrete usually equals death. If you want to avoid the slam, you have to instinctively grab your opponent's leg.

MMA Tactics

When you bring up the Rubber Guard in the same sentence as Mixed Martial Arts competition, there are a lot of people out there who have strong feelings. The majority of people who have studied the Rubber Guard consider it to be the best guard game out there. Those who live and die by tradition and don't take the time to learn what the system can offer them usually say the same thing—all you have to do to defend the Rubber Guard is stack your opponent or posture up and back out. I think these people are both right and retarded. They are right because if you aren't efficient with the Rubber Guard and your opponent is much stronger than you, there is a good possibility that he will be able to posture up and back out. They are right because a stronger opponent will be able to break your Rubber Guard by stacking you. They are retarded because there isn't a guard out there that is immune to either of these things. In the traditional guard an opponent can just as easily stack you. You can also get picked up and slammed. It's just the brutal nature of the guard.

It's these same retards that say you can get crushed by punches when playing the Rubber Guard. Once again, they are partially right. Is there a half guard out there that allows you to stop all punches and simulta-

neously sweep your opponent? I sure as hell haven't seen one. If you have such a guard, you should write a book and put out a DVD. I will buy both and become a huge fan. But up until now, I haven't met a jiu-jitsu practitioner with such a system. Nothing works a hundred percent of the time. If your opponents are always pulling out of your Rubber Guard, then you're not playing it right. Instead of going back to the drawing board and polishing your techniques, you could always do what many of the MMA fighters are doing and not even bother trying to break your opponent down. You could plant your feet on your opponent's hips, go to the double wrist-control guard, and then try to throw up a wild Triangle. It'll work every once in a while, but not that often. The Nogueira brothers who fight over in Japan are experts at this, but if you watch their recent fights, you'll see more and more opponents are learning how to counter their movement. You'll also see them get hit a lot. But does their style keep their opponent from posturing up and backing out? It would be great for the Nogueira brothers if it did, but it doesn't. It happens all the time when playing the double wrist-control guard.

You don't have to be a rocket scientist or a seasoned MMA athlete to understand that if you break your opponent down into the clinch it becomes much harder for him to punch you. It's pretty straightforward. Your opponent might land a few blows, but they are not going to be devastating shots. When using the double wrist-control guard, all your opponent has to do is circle his arm around and then drive in the punch. From the Rubber Guard clinch, usually the best he'll manage are little pitter-pat strikes. I'll let you decide which is better.

The Machete

If you take my advice and wear gi pants when you roll, you are going to want to learn this technique. Every time an opponent grabs your pants to help pass your guard, you want to hook his wrist with your forearm and then curl your arm back into your body. Once you get this down, you will no longer have a problem with opponents using your pants to help them pass your guard.

Einstein grabs hold of my gi pants to help him pass my guard.

I chop my left forearm into Einstein's right wrist.

To break Einstein's right grip on my gi pants, I curl my arm into my body.

Still pulling Einstein's right arm into my body, I move my right hand towards his left arm to break his second grip.

I chop my right arm into Einstein's left wrist.

Drawing my right arm into my body, I have broken both of Einstein's grips and prevented him from passing my guard.

Transition to Dogfight

As I mentioned in the introduction, you must learn how to jump back and forth between the Rubber Guard, the half guard, and the butterfly guard in order to develop a dangerous guard game. Here I am showing you how to go from full guard to half guard, and then from half guard up into the Dogfight position. This technique comes in handy when you simply can't break your opponent down into your guard. You tried every technique I've laid out, but your opponent's defenses are just too sharp. Instead of just lying there, waiting for your opponent to pass, you head over to the Dogfight to do battle from there. If nothing is working for you in the Dogfight, you head somewhere else. Because everything is connected in my system, you never have to abandon your offense.

I attempt to sit up to break Compella down into my guard, but his posture and base are too strong.

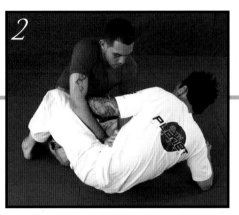

Instead of wasting energy trying to break Compella down, I decide to transition to the Dogfight position. Unhooking my legs, I post on my right elbow and reach my left arm underneath Compella's right arm. At the same time, I drive my right foot between Compella's legs.

As I slip my left arm deeper around Compella's back, I secure his right leg in the Lockdown.

With the Lockdown secure, I whip up to my right side. If you are uncertain as to your options from here, revisit the half guard section.

Driving down with my under-hook, I release the Lockdown and come up to my knees.

As I come all the way up to my knees, I keep my body pressed tightly against Compella's body and maintain a deep under-hook. Notice how I have hooked my left leg under Compella's right instep and sat back. This prevents him from escaping. It also prevents him from getting butterfly guard or full guard if he should turn into me. If you are uncertain as to your options from here, revisit the Dogfight section.

The Stack Attack

When you have an opponent in your guard and he stands up to stack you, his base will be compromised. As long as you always anticipate the stack, you can turn the situation to your favor. You do this by sweeping him over the moment he stands up. It's not a simple task to achieve; you must drill this sweep just like you do any other. Simply glancing over the move to learn how it's done is not enough. If you're not ready to counter the instant your opponent beings to stand, you run the risk of getting your guard passed.

I've broken Laurence down into Mission Control.

Laurence gets up to his feet and stacks me by driving his head and weight downward.

With Laurence driving all his weight downward, it becomes very hard for me to maintain Mission Control.

I hook my right foot around the inside of Laurence's left leg, securing a butterfly hook.

As I lift Laurence's left leg up and over with my right butterfly hook, I chop my left heel into the outside of his right knee. Then I scissor my legs to sweep him over to his back.

As I follow Laurence over, I keep my left leg hooked around his right leg and my right leg hooked around his left leg. It is important that you really drive your right leg down to the mat to limit your opponent's ability to scramble.

I land in the mount position.

To secure the mount position, I slide my left arm underneath Laurence's head and clasp my hands together using a Gable Grip under his left shoulder. I also bring my left knee up and dig it underneath his right shoulder. To learn about your options from here, purchase Mastering the Twister.

The Drop Kick

This is another option to sweep your opponent when he stacks you in the Rubber Guard. It's best utilized when your opponent's weight is centered over the top of you. It can be a little risky because it requires that you balance your opponent's weight as you lift him off the mat, but If your opponent shifts to one side in the middle of the technique, you can make a rather simple transition to the Stack Attack.

I've broken Laurence down into Mission Control.

Laurence gets up to his feet and stacks me by driving his head and weight downward.

With Laurence driving all his weight downward, it becomes very hard for me to maintain Mission Control.

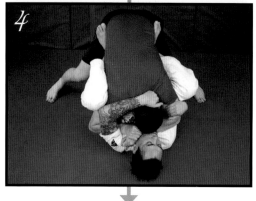

I drop my left foot to Laurence's right hip, wrap my left arm around the back of his neck, and grab his left biceps with my right hand. The last two of these three actions are to stop Laurence from being able to posture up as I lift him off the mat.

I launch Laurence into the air by rolling onto my upper back and driving my feet up into his hips. Laurence manages to free his right arm and post it on the mat, but because I have maintained control of his head and left arm, he is powerless to stop the sweep.

I continue to drive Laurence over using my feet.

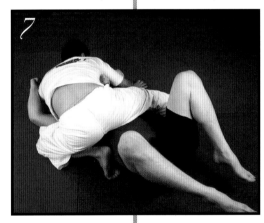

Using my grip on Laurence's head, I follow him all the way over and claim the mount position.

Because I already have my left arm wrapped underneath Laurence's head, all I have to do to establish the mount position is slide my right arm under his left arm and lock my hands together under his right shoulder using a Gable Grip.

Cock Block

Getting picked up and then slammed back down is not the most enjoyable thing out there. In order to avoid these painful free falls, you must become a master at hooking your opponent's leg the moment he stands up. If you hook his leg properly and he doesn't drop back down to his knees, it sets you up perfectly for a sweep. For those of you who plan on competing in MMA, I highly recommend that you put some serious time into drilling this technique.

I've broken Einstein down into Mission Control.

Einstein gets up to his feet. I know he is either trying to break my open guard or pick me up and slam me, neither of which is good.

As Einstein stands up, I hook my left arm around the outside of his right leg.

Bringing up my right leg, I hook my right foot over the top of my left foot to establish Crack Head Control. This is a much stronger control position and makes it very hard for Einstein to pick me up.

Einstein realizes that if he were to remain on his feet he would not only burn energy, but also run the risk of getting swept. He opts to drop back down to his knees.

I now have Einstein broken down in Crack Head Control.

The Pump Off The Stack

Sometimes executing the regular Pump can be difficult because you don't have the space needed to shove your opponent's elbow into the middle of your stomach. It's actually sometimes easier to execute the Pump when your opponent stands up to stack you. Instead of inching his elbow toward the center of you stomach by pumping your hips into him, you want to blast him up using your legs the moment he begins to stand. This allows you to get his elbow in and secure a deep hook on his arm.

I've broken Einstein down into Mission Control.

Einstein comes up onto his left foot. The moment he does this, I swing my right leg up to establish Crack Head Control.

Hooking my right foot over the top of my left, I secure Crack Head Control. Determined to get the slam, Einstein comes up to both feet, driving his weight forward to stack me.

Einstein postures up in an attempt to pick me up and slam me back down. As he does this, I place my left hand on his right elbow.

Using my left hand, I drive Einstein's right elbow across my midsection. Once I have his elbow to the center of my body, I slide my left arm over his right arm, making sure to hook the crook of my elbow over the crook of his elbow. To ensure my over-hook remains tight for the duration of the technique, I latch onto my right hip with my left hand.

I unhook my right hand from my left leg.

I reach my right arm down and hook it around the inside of Einstein's left leg.

MASTERING THE RUBBER GUARD

8

I use my right under-hook to help spin my body in a counterclockwise direction. Although I unhook my legs, I continue to curl my legs down into Einstein to prevent him from posturing up. It is important to notice how my left knee is touching the side of his head.

9

As I spin, I place my left leg on the left side of Einstein's face.

10

Now that I've completed my rotation, I C-cup the back of Einstein's left knee with my right hand. To roll him over to his back, I drop my left leg to the mat to generate momentum and drive my right leg into Einstein's side. To help his roll along, I guide his left leg over with my right hand.

11

As Einstein rolls onto his back, I establish the Spider Web position by hooking my left leg over his head and locking my feet together under his left shoulder. To prevent him from scrambling away, I wrap my arm around his right leg. To learn your options from this position, see the Spider Web section.

The Noogie Control

For those of you competing in mixed martial arts competition, remember that when utilizing the Rubber Guard system you will usually have a free hand to punch with. You can use strikes to help make the transition from Mission Control to New York, New York to Chill Dog, and Chill Dog to Jiu-Claw. In this particular sequence, I'm utilizing punches to distract my opponent so I can trap his hand to the mat.

I've got Compella broken down into Mission Control.

I attempt to get Compella's hand to the mat utilizing The Zombie, but his defense is too tight.

Taking advantage of my free left hand, I wind my fist back to punch Compella in face.

The hammer of destruction is getting closer to Compella's face.

Contact! Just socked Compella in the ear.

I draw back the hammer of death once again.

Wham! This one lands to the temple.

Compella attempts to retaliate with a punch of his own. With his left arm trapped against my chest, he throws a looping right hand at my face. This is the exact reaction I was hoping for because it gives me an opportunity to secure his hand to the mat.

I block Compella's punch by lifting my left arm. It is important to notice that I'm sliding my elbow up toward the inside of his elbow.

I hook my left arm around Compella's arm. Notice how this forces his hand toward the mat.

Now that I've forced Compella's hand to the mat, I trap it there by wrapping my left arm around my left knee. This lands me in New York.

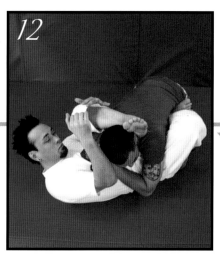

While Compella is still trying to figure out what just happened, I quickly move my right arm to the right side of his head.

I reach the Chill Dog position by hooking my right wrist over my left leg. To learn your options from here, revisit the section devoted to Chill Dog.

Crack Bows

Sometimes it's difficult to execute The Pump from Crack Head Control because your opponent won't let you push his arm toward the center of your chest. If you are competing in or training for mixed martial arts competition, you can distract your opponent by socking him in the face. Once you start raining down blows, your opponent will most likely bring his hands up to protect himself. This gives you an opportunity to push his elbow toward the center of your chest and move right into The Pump.

I've broken Einstein down into Mission Control.

Pushing off Einstein's left hip, I bring my right leg up to establish Crack Head Control.

Hooking my right foot over my left to secure Crack Head Control, I immediately try to push Einstein's elbow toward the center of my body using my left hand. If I can achieve this goal, I can utilize The Pump.

Einstein's elbow won't budge because his defense is sharp. I decide to use my free hand to throw some punches, hoping to break his defenses down. I coil my left hand back.

I sock Einstein in the ear. It's not a powerful blow because I have no leverage, but it gets his attention.

As I draw my fist back to land another punch, Einstein attempts to block the punch by putting his hands up to the right side of is head.

By putting his hands up to block my punch, Einstein is giving me an opportunity to push his elbow in and utilize The Pump.

I shove Einstein's right elbow toward the center of my body using my left hand.

Once I get Einstein's elbow in, I secure a tight over-hook with my left arm. I do this by sliding my left arm over Laurence's right arm and underneath his left arm.

To lock my hook on Einstein's arm tight, I grab hold of my right hip with my left hand.

I bring my right arm down and reach back for Einstein's left leg.

I hook my right arm around the inside of Einstein's left leg, and then use that hook to spin my hips in a counterclockwise direction. Notice how this puts my body at a forty-five degree angle with Einstein's body, which allows me to attack his right arm.

I wrap my left leg around the left side of Einstein's head. To sweep him over to his back, I apply downward pressure with both legs. My left leg drives into the side of Einstein's head, and my right leg drives into his left side. To help cast him over, I also C-cup my right hand around the inside of his left knee and push his leg upward. When done right, your opponent won't be able to resist the roll.

I maintain control of Laurence's body as he rolls over onto his back by squeezing my knees together, curling my legs tight over his body and head, and keeping my deep hook on his right arm super tight.

Without any hesitation, I wrap my right arm around Laurence's right leg to prevent a scramble. I now have Laurence in the Spider Web position. To learn your options from here, visit the Spider Web section.

Chill Bows

When trying to transition from Chill Dog to Jiu-Claw, it can sometimes be difficult to free your leg from underneath your opponent using the Kung Fu Move. Mad Dog Control and the Crowbar are two techniques you can utilize when the Kung Fu Move isn't working, but if you are competing in a mixed martial arts competition that allows elbow strikes, you have another great option at your disposal. By driving powerful elbows into your opponent's head, you can usually create enough space to pull your leg out from underneath him and transition into Jiu-Claw.

I've got Compella in Chill Dog.

Using my right hand, I pull my left leg to the front of Compella's face.

I release my right grip on my leg and place my palm against my ankle. I then execute the Kung Fu Move by using my right hand to drive my left foot into Compella's face.

Compella knows that I'm trying to reach the Jiu-Claw control position. To prevent me from accomplishing this, he latches firmly onto my right leg. To counter his defense I could utilize the Crowbar or Mad Dog Control, but instead I draw my right arm back to land elbow strikes to his head.

I land a solid elbow to Compella's ear.

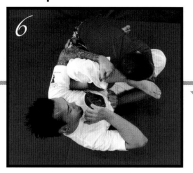

I draw my right elbow back to land another blow.

Not wanting to get struck again, Compella turns away from me. The moment he does this, I rotate in a clockwise direction, grab his right wrist with my right hand, and reach my left arm around the back of his legs.

I've established the Jiu-Claw control position. To see your options from here, revisit the Jiu-Claw section.

Part Five
SPIDER WEB

Introduction to the Spider Web

I would rather be in the Spider Web than have my opponent's back. That's how dominant of a position it is. For me it's not just a dead zone; it's the best dead zone. When you have your opponent's back, he has his hands, his chin, and his shoulders to defend against the choke. In the Spider Web, the only thing your opponent can do to hinder you from attacking his arm is clasp his hands together. That single grip is all he has. As long as you have a really deep hook on his arm, that grip is not hard to break.

Of course you must still learn the proper way to set up your submissions. In addition to hooking your opponent's arm, you must also wrap your opposite hand around your opponent's leg. This prevents him from being able to get to his knees and crawl back into your guard, as well as from kneeing you in the head. A lot of jiu-jitsu practitioners will let go of their opponent's leg when they go for a submission, but I prefer to hang onto that leg whenever possible. Al-though this requires that you learn how to finish your opponent with one arm, it ensures that he will remain on his back. There are finishes that require both arms, but you should utilize those as a last resort. You always want to maintain control of your opponent, and when the Spider Web is played correctly, your control is phenomenal. In fact, it offers so much control that I personally feel everyone should learn five to ten different paths that will get them to the Spider Web. In addition to getting there from the guard, you can get there from the mount, the back, and from side control, all of which is laid out in Mastering the Twister. In order to fully take full advantage of one of the most dominant positions in jiu-jitsu, it is important to learn as many routes to the Spider Web as possible.

Arm Crush

The Arm Crush, which I learned from Carlos Machado, is my most treasured technique from the Spider Web position. The reason I like it so much is that it plays right into my opponent's game plan, which is to keep his trapped arm bent at all costs. Instead of trying to wrestle his arm straight, which can be difficult with really strong opponents, I simply throw my leg over his bent arm and crush it. Once I have that vice locked tight, my opponent's game plan changes. He'll suddenly do everything in his power to straighten his arm and alleviate the pain. If there is a lot of sweat, sometimes he will be able to achieve his goal, but because I anticipate his escape, I can transition right into the regular Arm Bar. The key to improving your success rate with both techniques is to keep your free hand wrapped around your opponent's leg to stop him from escaping up to his knees. If you need two hands to execute either of these moves, you're doing them wrong.

I've got Laurence in the Spider Web position.

Unhooking my feet, I place my right leg on top of Laurence's right wrist.

I hook my left leg over the top of my right foot. Then I wedge my left foot underneath the back of Laurence's neck.

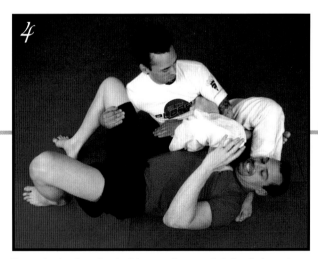

To apply the Arm Crush, I karate chop my left hand through my right thigh, draw my left elbow back, and turn my body in a counterclockwise direction. It is important to notice that my left palm is parallel with the mat.

Triangle Arm Bar

The way your opponent can block the Arm Crush is to elevate his arms off his chest. Although this makes it difficult to place your leg on top of his arms, it allows you to slip one leg underneath his arms and go for the Triangle Arm Bar. If you can't get the submission because the technique places you at an odd angle in relation to your opponent, which tends to happen on occasion, then you can keep your legs triangled and attack your opponent's arm..

I've got Laurence in the Spider Web position.

Sensing that I will attempt the Arm Crush, Laurence defends against the submission by raising his arms. Quickly adapting to the situation, I point the toes of my right foot and slip my leg into the gap that just opened beneath his arms.

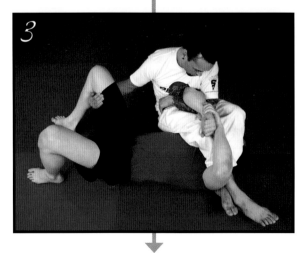

I slip my leg all the way through the gap and place my right foot over the top of my left.

Releasing my hold on Laurence's leg, I clasp my hands together using a Gable Grip. It is important to notice how tightly I'm controlling Laurence. I'm hugging his right arm to my chest using my arms and pinning his head and shoulders to the mat with my legs.

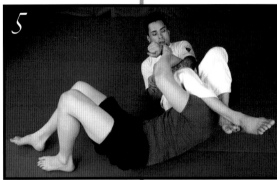

I roll to my back and pull Laurence with me.

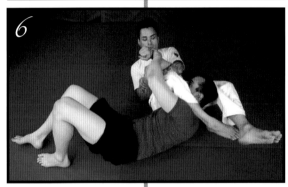

As I come down onto my back, I reposition my left leg to the back of Laurence's head.

To lock in the Triangle, I hook my left leg over my right foot, flex my toes, and squeeze my knees together.

I secure the Triangle Arm Bar by pulling my arms toward my head to break Laurence's grip, sliding my hands up to his wrist, elevating my hips, and then pulling his arm toward my chest.

The Slide

The Slide works wonderfully from the Spider Web position when your opponent is determined to make it up to his knees. As long as you've got one arm hooking his leg and you've got a deep hook on his other arm, it will be very difficult for your opponent to achieve his goal. As you drop back he will most likely try to reach his knees, and that is when you slide your arm up to his wrist and leg curl him back down. This shatters his grip and allows you to apply the arm bar.

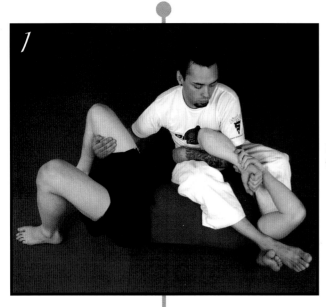

I've got Laurence in the Spider Web.

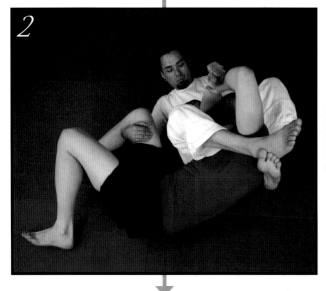

I roll to my back and pull Laurence with me using my deep hook on his right arm.

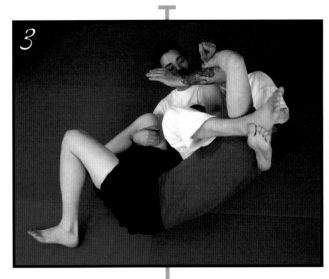

I slide my left elbow up to Laurence's right wrist.

To break Laurence's grip, I keep my left elbow tight to my body and begin to curl both legs toward the mat.

I continue to curl both legs toward the mat to pin Laurence's shoulders. To finish him with the Arm Bar, I maintain a deep hook on his right arm and arch my hips upward.

X-Break

The X-Break is another technique that allows you to break your opponent's grip without letting go of his leg. It works particularly well on opponents who have a really strong hand clasp. To reach your goal of shattering his grip and straightening his arm, you position your feet in such a way that allows you to drive his arm away from you. At the same time, you pull his trapped arm into you. If your opponent has a freakishly strong grip, sometimes you will need to employ both arms. However, this requires that you let go of your opponent's leg, which gives him an opportunity to blast up to his knees. When using both hands, speed is of the essence. I learned this technique from Gerald Strebendt, one of my top students.

I have Laurence in the Spider Web.

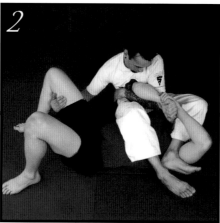

Sensing that I will attempt the Arm Crush, Laurence defends against the submission by elevating his arms. By taking this defensive action, Laurence has just created an opportunity for me to execute the X-Break. I begin by sliding my left leg underneath his arms and hooking my foot around his biceps.

With my left hook secure, I slide my right leg over the top of my left.

I hook my right foot around the opposite side of Laurence's biceps.

I break Laurence's grip by extending both legs and leaning back. It is important that you keep your deep hook super tight, pinching your opponent's arm with the inside of your elbow. This will not only insure that you keep his arm trapped, but it will also ensure that the thumb of his trapped arm remains pointing up, which is required for the submission to work properly.

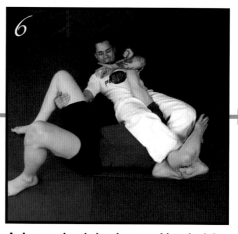

As Laurence's grip breaks apart, I lean back further and slide my left arm up to his wrist. Keeping my deep hook tight, I arch my hips upward and force Laurence to submit from the Arm Bar. It is important to notice how I have kept my right hand hooked around Laurence's leg for the duration of the move to prevent a scramble.

The Filho

I saw Brazilian Top Team member Paulo Filho execute this technique from the Spider Web in the Pride Fighting Championships. His opponent had his hands gripped together as though his life depended upon it, making it very hard for Filho to break his grip. Did Filho let go of his opponent's leg so he could employ both arms? No. Instead he laid down on his side and sunk his arm super deep around his opponent's leg. This allowed him to use both hands to break his opponent's grip and still maintain control of his opponent's leg. A few days after I saw the technique, I tried it out in training and it worked quite well. It has been a part of my game ever since.

I've got Laurence trapped in the Spider Web.

I roll onto my right side, pulling Laurence with me using my deep hook on his arm. As I do this, I hook my right arm deeper around his right leg.

Hooking my right arm all the way around Laurence's right leg, I grab his right wrist with my right hand.

Still controlling Laurence's wrist, I place my left foot left foot on his left biceps.

I use my left foot to drive Laurence's shoulders to the mat. Because I have tight control on his right wrist, it tears his grip apart.

Now that I have broken Laurence's grip, I lock my left arm to my chest and fall back. Keeping downward pressure on Laurence's left biceps, I apply the Arm Lock by squeezing my knees together and arching my hips upward.

Chamber Lock

The Chamber Lock is a variation of the Arm Crush that my student Jason Chambers came up with. It looks very unorthodox because you're essentially putting yourself in a toehold, but it puts a tremendous amount of pressure on your opponent's arm. I don't use it that much because I don't like letting go of my opponent's leg, and when I do let go of his leg, it's usually because I'm attempting the Silverado. However, Jason gets taps all the time using this technique. It's a great option to have in your bag of tricks.

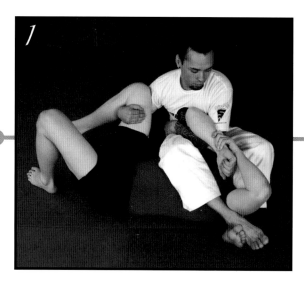

I've got Laurence trapped in the Spider Web.

Unhooking my feet, I place my left leg over the top of Laurence's right wrist.

Releasing my hook on Laurence's leg, I grip the top of my left foot with my right hand. It is important to note that anytime you release your opponent's leg in the Spider Web position, he will have a small window of opportunity to force a scramble. For this reason, you must perform this last step before your opponent realizes what is going on.

As I pull my left foot down with my right hand, I grip my right wrist with my left hand. Then I drive my left arm up, using my grip for leverage. This crushes Laurence's arm and forces him to tap.

The Silverado

This is a technique that a Brazilian named Silvio Pamento showed me at Jean Jacques' academy back when he was a purple belt. After getting to know him, I realized where he must have gotten it. Shortly after migrating from Brazil to America, he earned a black belt under Gene Lebell. It's probably an old school judo move that has a traditional name, but I'm no good at remember names like that. The reason I call it the Silverado is because that's what Lebell always called Silvio. I guess he had trouble remembering the guy's real name. As for the move, I go to it all the time when none of my other moves are working. The reason I use it as a last resort is because it requires that you let go of your opponent's leg.

I've got Laurence trapped in the Spider Web.

As I sit forward, I slide my left arm up to Laurence's right wrist and hook my left hand around the outside of my right knee.

Releasing my hold on Laurence's leg, I bring my right elbow over the top of his right arm.

Having slid my left arm up to Laurence's wrist, I have room to wedge my right elbow against the backside of his right arm.

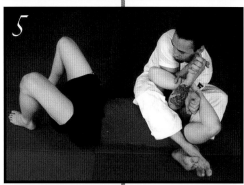

I lift my left arm and clasp my hands together using a reverse Gable Grip. Notice how I now have Laurence's right arm trapped between my arms.

Pinching my elbows together, I sit up and twist my shoulders in a counterclockwise direction to break Laurence's grip.

Once I break Laurence's grip, I lean back and slide both of my hands up to his wrist.

To apply the Arm Lock, I squeeze my knees together, extend my hips upward, and pull Laurence's arm to my chest.

Part Six
ESCAPES TO GUARD

Introduction to Escapes to Guard

Another reason you should spend some time perfecting your half guard game is because the half guard is usually just a few step away, making it a great position to retreat to when your opponent manages to obtain dominant positioning. In this section I will show techniques that allow you to escape back to the half guard when your opponent claims your back, the mount, or side control. Most people don't take the time to learn these options because they don't have a strong half guard, but if you've read and studied this book from the start, you won't have this problem. Learning the upcoming techniques will give you a whole mess of options from disadvantageous positions where your options are generally few.

To make the most of the techniques I offer, you should always be thinking about establishing double under-hooks and whipping up to your side while making your escape because it sometimes allows you to catch your opponent off guard. While he is still focused on trying to maintain the mount, side control, or your back, you're reaching your basic goals that put you into a position to attack.

Not all of your escapes to the half guard will work a hundred percent of the time. I've only included the escapes that I've had a success with, but you should still experiment as much as possible to find out what works best for you. If an escape attempt fails and your opponent ends up in side control, that isn't always a bad thing, especially if you were escaping the mount or back. The key to success when it comes to escapes to half guard is putting in the numbers. You could have the most dangerous half guard in the world, but it will do little good unless you can get there.

I've also included escapes to butterfly guard and escapes to full guard. As I mentioned in the introduction, the key to mastering the Rubber Guard is learning how to move back and forth between the different positions. Once you achieve that skill, it becomes a lot harder for your opponent to shut down your offense.

T-Rex

When you're lying on your back, you never want to let your elbows get too far away from your body because it gives your opponent an opportunity to attack your arms. Letting your elbows hang out won't increase your offense or defense, so don't do it. You also don't want your elbows too close together because it weakens your defense. If your opponent is mounted, having your elbows too close together allows him to walk his knees up to your armpits, which is disastrous. If your opponent is in side control, it allows him to bring his knees closer to your body. The T-Rex is a very important aspect of defense when you're on the bottom, and much attention should be paid to it. I'm always surprised at how many advanced jiu-jitsu practitioners forget such a simple concept.

Having assumed the T-Rex position, my arms are up and my elbows are pressed tightly against my ribs. My palms are facing each other for safety and mobility. My shoulders are off the mat, and my chin is tucked to protect my neck.

Escape From Alcatraz

There are several different techniques I use to escape to the half guard when mounted, but this is usually the one I will utilize first. It's a super strong move because it lands you in the half guard with the double under-hooks, and as you probably realize by now, that is huge. However, there are a few things you should pay attention to. If your opponent's arms are positioned up by your armpits, it will make it very difficult for you to turn on your side and hook his leg with your foot. In such a scenario, you will have to really make use of the T-Rex by driving his hips down with your elbows. Once you manage that, the key to making a successful escape is to flow all the way through the technique. If you pause, stop, or skip a step, your escape attempt will most likely fail.

Einstein is mounted on top of me. Although I have several options, I decide to use Escape From Alcatraz to escape to half guard.

I assume the T-Rex position by tucking my elbows to my ribs and my chin to my chest. As I do this, I turn over to my left side by straightening my left leg and pushing off the mat with my right foot. This allows me to curl my body in tight and wedge my elbows to the inside of Einstein's right hip and leg.

Driving Einstein's right leg away from my body using my elbows, I scoop my right foot underneath his right instep.

Using my right foot and elbows, I elevate Einstein's right leg. This allows me to slide my left leg underneath his right leg. It is important that you make the transition to the Lockdown quickly because there will be a small window of opportunity for your opponent to escape.

I wrap my left leg over Einstein's right leg, and then I hook my left foot under my right leg. Now that I've secured the Lockdown, Einstein will have a hard time escaping my half guard.

Dropping my feet to the mat, I position my arms in the T-Rex position and begin turning to my right side.

Still turning to my right side, I scoop my left arm underneath Einstein's right arm to establish an under-hook.

I reach my right hand underneath Einstein's left arm and lock my hands together behind his back using a Gable Grip. It is important to notice that I've positioned my grip just above Einstein's right hip.

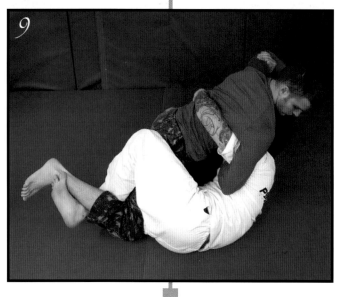

Einstein lifts his left arm to punch me in the face. To avoid his downward strike, I release my Gable Grip and place my right hand on his left biceps. It is important to notice that I've latched my left hand onto his left hip to keep my under-hook secure. Although gripping your opponent's biceps doesn't offer optimum control, it comes in handy to avoid punches when competing in Mixed Martial Arts Competition.

Guantanamo

This technique is very similar to the previous one. The main difference is that instead of hooking your foot underneath your opponent's leg, you step your foot over his leg. All the things you had to pay attention to with the last move apply to this one as well. If your opponent's hips are high, use the T-Rex to push them down. If your opponent has a grapevine on your legs, find a way to break them free. Don't stop, pause, or skip a step because it will give your opponent a chance to counter your escape. Explosion and speed are key. This is one of Jean Jacques' favorite escapes from the mount.

Einstein is mounted on top of me. Although I have several options, I decide to use the Guantanamo to escape to half guard.

I assume the T-Rex position by tucking my elbows to my ribs and my chin to my chest. As I do this, I turn over to my left side by straightening my left leg and pushing off the mat with my right foot. Notice how I curl my body in tight. This prevents Einstein from being able to flatten me out by dropping his weight.

While maintaining the T-Rex position, I step my right foot over Einstein's right leg. Immediately I drive my right heel into the open space between the top of his foot and the mat. This allows me to hook his right leg with my right foot.

Curling my right heel towards my buttocks, I trap Einstein's right foot in the crook of my knee. Using that hook, I pull Einstein's leg toward my right side. It is important that you maintain constant pressure with your hook. If you don't, your opponent will be able to pull his trapped leg free.

Turning my body toward my right side, I slide my right foot under my left and straighten out my legs. To keep Einstein from being able to pull his trapped leg free, I squeeze my knees together as tightly as possible. It is important to notice that my arms are still in the T-Rex position.

As I turn onto my right side, I unhook my feet and shrimp my hips out to my left. This opens a window for Einstein to escape, so I must secure the Lockdown as quickly as possible.

I secure the Lockdown by hooking my right foot underneath Einstein's right instep, sliding my left leg over the top of Einstein's right leg, and then hooking my left foot underneath my right leg.

Keeping my body curled tight, I reach my left arm around Einstein's body and secure a deep under-hook. To disrupt Einstein's base, I squeeze my knees together and straighten my legs.

As I stretch Einstein out with the Lockdown, he postures up to reestablish his base. This creates the space I need to whip up to my side and secure a Gable Grip. From here I have multiple sweeps at my disposal.

Einstein lifts his left hand to punch me in the head. To avoid his downward strike, I release my Gable Grip and place my right hand on his left biceps. It is important to notice that I've latched my left hand onto his left hip to keep my under-hook secure. Although gripping your opponent's biceps doesn't offer optimum control, it comes in handy when competing in Mixed Martial Arts Competition.

Hip Escape

When the previous two mount escapes fail, I'll resort to this one. It's not any less effective than the other two; it's just the escape that everyone expects. They expect it because it's so simple. All it entails is shrimping over to your side and sliding your leg underneath your opponent's leg, which puts you in the half guard. Although this seems quite easy, it can sometimes be a battle. If your opponent has a really good mount, you might have to swivel your hips back and forth to get your leg underneath his. Once you get that leg under, you must be quick to secure the Lockdown. Your opponent will realize that the mount is lost and he might try to bail out into side control. If your opponent manages to get side control, you still accomplished something. You just escaped a very bad position, and now you can work to get to half guard from side control, which is a whole lot easier.

Einstein is mounted on top of me. Although I have several options, I decide to shrimp my way to half guard.

I assume the T-Rex position by tucking my elbows to my ribs and my chin to my chest. As I do this, I turn over to my left side and curl my body in tight. This allows me to wedge my elbows to the inside of Einstein's right hip and leg.

Driving my right elbow into Einstein's right leg, I create the separation needed to slide my left leg under his right leg. It is important to notice how tightly I'm balled up; I've brought my left quadriceps all the way up to my elbows. If you do not remain balled up with your arms in the T-Rex position, your opponent will be able to reclaim the mount position.

Swiveling over to my back, I maintain separation by pressing on Einstein's right hip with both hands. If you do not keep that pressure, your opponent will be able to bring his right leg forward and reclaim the mount position.

Still pressing on Einstein's right hip with both hands, I shrimp my body out to my right.

To secure the Lockdown, I hook my right foot under Einstein's right instep, step my left leg over his right leg, and then hook my left foot underneath my right leg. Still rotating to my right side, I reach my left arm around Einstein's back to establish an under-hook.

I stretch Einstein out with the Lockdown by squeezing my knees together and straightening my legs. This disrupts his base and causes him to posture up. I quickly capitalize on the opportunity by sitting up and secure the double under-hooks.

25 Cent

Lying flat on your back when your opponent has side control is not the best position because your opponent is set up perfectly to attack. He has an assortment of submissions at his disposal or he can work to establish the mount. In such a situation, I'll try to come up to my side and face my opponent because it makes escaping to half guard a whole lot easier. If I can't come up to my side and face my opponent because he is pinning my shoulders to the mat with head and arm control, I'll utilize this technique. Although it won't get me to half guard with the double under-hooks, it will get me the Lockdown. I'll then have to engage in a whole new battle to get the double under-hooks and work up to my side, but I'll take that battle any day over being stuck in the bottom side control position. The key to being successful with this move is to quickly hook your opponent's leg. This requires that you drop your knee closest to your opponent to the mat, which destroys your defenses for a split second. If you are slow to hook your opponent's leg, he might realize that he has a window of opportunity to place his knee on your belly or transition to the mount.

Einstein is in side control, using his head and arm control to pin my shoulders to the mat. I've got my right knee elevated to prevent him from climbing into the mount.

Turning to my right side, I drop my right knee to the mat and bring my left leg over my right leg.

I step my left foot over Einstein's right leg, hooking my heel underneath his shin. To trap his right leg, I drive my left foot toward my right knee.

I scissor my legs by driving my left knee in a counterclockwise direction and my right knee in a clockwise direction. It is important to have proper positioning when you do this. Notice how my left knee is pulling on Einstein's ankle and my right knee is pushing into his knee. It is these two opposite forces that cause his leg to bend to the side. It is also important to notice that my left leg is still curled tight, preventing him from pulling his leg free.

Keeping my left leg curled in tight, I turn toward my left side. This pulls Einstein's right leg into my half guard.

With Einstein now in my half guard, I hook my left foot underneath my right leg. As I do this, Einstein's right knee is forced to the mat, which will help me secure the Lockdown.

I secure the Lockdown by hooking my right foot underneath Einstein's right leg. To destroy his posture, I pinch my knees together and straighten out my legs. Although from here I still have to establish the double under-hooks and whip up to my side, it is a hell of a lot better than being stuck in the bottom side control position.

The Flo

When done in one fluid motion, The Flo is an excellent way to escape the bottom side control position and secure the butterfly guard. If you don't do the move in one fluid motion, your opponent will have a window of opportunity to climb into the mount. Getting your first butterfly hook in is key—it's what shuts your opponent's mount opportunity down. You also need to keep your over-hook tight and push on your opponent's hip for the duration of the escape. It's called The Flo because my student, Felicia L. Oh, rips her opponents a new one with this technique on a regular basis.

Einstein is in side control, using his head and arm control to pin my shoulders to the mat.

Pushing off Einstein's left hip with my right hand, I create enough separation between our bodies to hook my left arm around his right arm.

Still pushing off Einstein's hip with my right hand, I turn onto my left hip, push off the mat with my left foot, and step my right leg over Einstein's right leg. It is important to notice that I'm using my over-hook to pull down on Einstein's right arm.

I hook my right foot around the inside of Einstein's right leg. I'm still pushing on his left hip with my right hand, as well as disrupting his base by pulling his left arm down with my right over-hook.

Lifting Einstein's right leg with my right foot, I slip my left knee underneath his right leg and hook my foot around the inside of his thigh. I'm still pushing on his hip to maintain hip separation, as well as keeping his weight forward using my over-hook. It is important to note that if you don't keep your over-hook tight, your opponent will have the opportunity to defend the escape by sitting back and reestablishing his base.

As I unhook my right leg, I lift Einstein's right leg up using my left butterfly hook. This creates enough room to slip my right leg underneath his body.

Driving Einstein's right leg upward with my left butterfly hook, I slide my right knee underneath his body and pull it out on the other side. Instead of sliding my right foot all the way out, I hook it around the inside of his left leg. With both butterfly hooks in, I slide my right hand up his back and establish a deep hook over his shoulder. Notice how I am currently lying flat on my back. In order to be offensive, I must sit up into the Cocoon position.

Stretching my legs out, I force Einstein's weight back. As he sits up to reestablish his base, I sit up with him and use my over-hook to pull my body close to his. From here, I can work for a sweep or transition.

The B. Smith

North South can be a dangerous position when you're on the bottom. If you are like me, you will prefer the half guard. Not only will this technique take you to half guard, but it will also give you the double under-hooks. The key to being successful with this move is to get your elbows into the T-Rex position, and then create separation by pushing on your opponent's hips. Once you create enough separation so that your opponent can no longer use his head to block your backward roll, kicking your legs over and establishing your hook shouldn't be that difficult. The nice thing about this technique is that your opponent will usually think you're trying to take his back. He'll be satisfied when you only get one hook, not realizing that's all you were going for in the first place. The reason I call it the B. Smith is because my student, Brad Smith, gets more mileage out of this move than anyone I know.

With Einstein on top of me in the north/south position, I'm determined to escape to half guard.

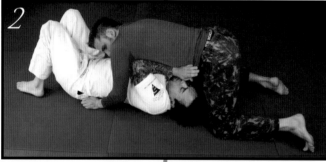

Bringing my elbows in tight to my body, I establish the T-Rex position.

I create separation between my head and Einstein's hips by placing my hands on his hips and pushing off.

Continuing to push off Einstein's hips with both hands, I cartwheel backwards. I throw my right leg up and over Einstein's left shoulder, and I throw my left leg over Einstein's left arm. Then I slip my left foot to the inside of his left hip. This entire motion is similar to doing a backwards roll over your left shoulder. However, there is one very important thing I must point out. Notice how both of my legs are to the left side of Einstein's head. If I hadn't cleared both of my legs around his head, Einstein could have rammed his head into my hips, neutralizing my escape.

I hook my left leg around the inside of Einstein's left leg. I then use that hook to rotate my body underneath him.

As I come down onto my left side, I slide my right arm underneath Einstein's left arm to establish an under-hook. I also change the positioning of my legs. In the previous photo I had my left leg hooked around Einstein's left leg. Here I release that hook in order to step my right foot to the inside of Einstein's left leg. It is important not to release your left hook until your right foot is positioned to take its place. If you allow your opponent to free his leg, he gains the ability to step his left leg over your right leg and move into side control. You don't want that to happen, so make the switch quick and seamless.

To secure the Lockdown, I slide my left leg over my right foot, and then hook my left foot underneath Einstein's left foot. To stretch Einstein out and shatter his base, I pinch my knees together and straighten my legs.

I sit up with Einstein and clasp my hands together just below his rib cage using a Gable Grip. To keep him off balance, I continue to pinch my knees together and stretch him out with the Lockdown.

Einstein lifts his right hand to punch me in the head. To avoid his downward strike, I release my Gable Grip and place my left hand on his right biceps. It is important to notice that I've latched my right hand onto his right hip to keep my under-hook secure. Although gripping your opponent's biceps doesn't offer optimum control, it comes in handy to avoid punches when competing in Mixed Martial Arts Competition.

ESCAPES TO GUARD |

The JJ Back Escape

This technique should be utilized when an opponent has your back but only one hook. Jean Jacques showed me this move, and it's become my number one back escape. It doesn't always land me in half guard. Sometimes I end up in butterfly guard, and sometimes I end up getting mounted. It works not because it always gets me to half guard, but rather because it nearly always gets my opponent off my back, which is the position I least like to be in. I would much rather be mounted than have my opponent riding on my back because it is much easier to transition to the half guard from the mount.

Einstein is on my back with one hook, working for the choke. I defend the choke by pulling his arm away from my throat with my hands, tucking my chin to my chest, and turning both my body and head into Einstein's left arm. To counter my defense, Einstein tries to wrap his right leg around the inside of my right leg, which would give him a second hook and make it much easier to finish the choke. I stop him from achieving his goal by keeping my right knee high, essentially creating a barrier.

Still defending the choke, I roll into Einstein's left arm and up to my knees. To prevent him from securing his second hook, I keep my right knee tucked up by my chest.

Continuing to roll, I hook my left leg over the top of Einstein's left foot. At this point, I'm no longer in danger of being choked. Einstein is trying to climb into the mount position, but I'm preventing him from doing so with my left hook on his right leg.

Einstein is forced to release his chokehold as I continue to turn into him and use the ground to scrap him off my back. The moment he does this, I begin to reach my right arm underneath his left arm to establish an under-hook.

Still turning into Einstein, I step my right foot to the inside of his left knee. It is important to note that this step, as with all the steps in this escape, must be done consecutively. If you hesitate for even a moment, your opponent will have the opportunity to reclaim your back or transition into side control or the mount.

I secure the Lockdown by sliding my left leg over my right foot, and then hooking my left foot underneath Einstein's left leg. At the same time, I reach my right arm around Einstein's back to establish an under-hook.

Whipping up to my left side, I secure a Gable Grip just below Einstein's rib cage and squeeze my arms tight.

Einstein lifts his right hand to punch me in the head. To avoid his downward strike, I release my Gable Grip and place my left hand on his right biceps. It is important to notice that I've latched my right hand onto his right hip to keep my under-hook secure. Although gripping your opponent's biceps doesn't offer optimum control, it comes in handy to avoid punches when competing in Mixed Martial Arts Competition.

Hip Push Escape

Escaping to butterfly guard is always a good option when mounted. You not only escape a very bad position, but you're also setting yourself up to sweep your opponent or make the transition into the Pyramid or X-Guard. This particular escape requires that you heft your opponent's weight off you so you can wedge your knees between his legs and secure your butterfly hooks. When going up against an opponent who is lighter than you, it is possible to simply bench press his body upward. However, getting in the habit of elevating your opponent this way can get you into trouble when you go up against a heavier opponent. For this reason, it is best to heft your opponent using your hips and legs in addition to your arms. Even if your arms are super strong, it will conserve energy.

With Laurence mounted on top of me, I'm determined to escape.

I drive Laurence's hips toward my feet using my hands.

Extending my arms into Laurence's hips, I push off the mat with both legs and explode my hips to the sky.

Keeping Laurence's body up with my hands, I drop my hips to the mat. This allows me to draw my knees up and secure the butterfly guard.

Worried about being swept, Laurence bases back. I quickly sit up into him, wrapping my left arm over his right arm to secure an over-hook. Now that I'm in the Cocoon, I'm ready to attack.

MASTERING THE RUBBER GUARD

Shrimp Escape

When mounted, the Shrimp Escape can be an excellent tool to reach the butterfly guard. The key to being successful with this move is to keep shrimping back and forth, slowly working your opponent's hips down toward your legs. Your opponent will probably try to drive his hips forward, but this is positive in the regard that it will shut down his ability to attack. This takes away a major worry, and if you maintain your shrimping efforts, you'll eventually get one step ahead of him and be able to work your knees up and obtain the butterfly position.

With Laurence mounted on top of me, I'm determined to escape.

Pushing off my right foot, I turn onto my left side. At the same time, I drive my elbows into Laurence's right hip. The more separation I can create between Laurence's right leg and my body, the easier it will be to draw my left knee up from between his legs.

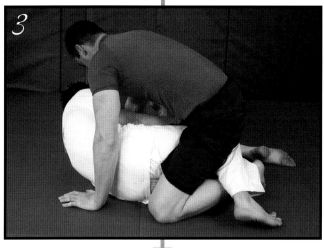

Continuing to drive my elbows into Laurence's right hip, I create the space needed to pull my left knee out from between his legs. Sometimes this comes easy, and sometimes it requires a good amount of elbow grease. Once I punch my knee through, I hook my left foot around the inside of his thigh to establish my first butterfly hook.

Using my left butter-fly hook for leverage, I shrimp towards my right side.

Planting both hands on Laurence's left thigh and pushing off, I pull my right knee up from between his legs. Notice how I scoot my hips back each time I shrimp over to my side. This will create extra space between you and your opponent, making it easier to draw your knees up.

Now that I have both butter-fly hooks established, Lau-rence worries about getting swept. The moment he sits his weight back and postures up, I come up with him and establish an over-hook on his right arm. This puts me in the Cocoon.

The Jailbreak

This technique, as well as the Jailbreak Variation, came in extremely handy when I went up against Royler Gracie in Abu Dhabi. As a matter of fact, it was these two techniques that allowed me to beat him. I went for the standard Jailbreak a couple of times, and then I executed the Jailbreak Variation. It took me to the Cocoon, I fake butterfly swept him, and he based out. The moment he did that, I went right through the Pyramid and into the Triangle. A few moments later, he was tapping in submission.

Einstein is in side control, using his head and arm control to pin my shoulders to the mat.

I push on Einstein's right hip with my left hand and secure an over-hook on his left arm. Notice how I bring my left knee up into his ribs to keep him from advancing into the mount.

Letting go of my over-hook, I grab my right foot with my right hand and pull it toward my head. As I do this, I keep my left knee planted in Einstein's ribs to prevent him from advancing into the mount. I also push off his right hip with my left hand to keep him from floating into the north/south position.

I secure a butterfly hook by shoving my right foot to the inside of Einstein's hip using my hand. It's important to notice that I'm still pushing on Einstein's right hip and keeping my left knee planted into his side.

Driving up with my butterfly hook, I create enough space to drag my left leg underneath my right.

Still driving up with my right butterfly hook to create separation, I punch my left knee underneath Einstein's body and hook my left foot around the inside of his right thigh.

Einstein sits back to reestablish his base. Keeping my right over-hook tight, I sit up with him and secure an under-hook with my left arm. Now that I'm in the Cocoon position, I'm ready to attack.

MASTERING THE RUBBER GUARD

The Jailbreak Variation

This variation of the Jailbreak comes in handy when the arm you've established your over-hook with is trapped between you and your opponent, making it impossible to grab your foot. Instead of trying to free that arm, you reach your opposite arm underneath your opponent, latch onto your foot, and then pull your foot to the inside of your opponent's hip. Speed is of the essence with this technique because you will no longer have your hand posted on your opponent's hip, which means he can make the transition to the north/south position if he senses your intentions. You have to reach under his body, grab your foot, get your hook, and then pull that hand back out to block his hip. There can be no hesitation. I know this technique works because it's what allowed me to defeat Royler Gracie in Abu Dhabi.

Einstein is in side control, pinning my shoulders to the mat using his head and arm control.

I push on Einstein's left hip with my right hand and secure an over-hook on his right arm. Notice how I have my right knee planted against Einstein's ribs. I will keep that knee up for the duration of the move to prevent him from advancing into the mount position.

Einstein drives his weight into me, trapping my left hand between our bodies. This makes the standard Jailbreak hard to manage, so I resort to the Jailbreak Variation by sliding my right hand underneath Einstein's body, grabbing hold of my left foot, and pulling it towards his right hip. I do this as quickly as possible because I no longer have my right hand on his hip, which means Einstein could potentially move into the north/south position by rotating his body in a clockwise direction.

The moment I hook my left foot around the inside of Einstein's right hip, I pull my right arm out from underneath his body and resume pushing on his left hip, making it hard for him to float into the North/South position.

Using my left butterfly hook to lift Einstein's hips up and away from me, I create enough space to slip my right knee underneath my left leg. To help punch my right knee through to the other side, I rotate my hips into Einstein. Notice how I am pulling on his left arm to help with the rotation.

Continuing to spin my hips into Einstein, I pull my right knee out on the opposite side. Instead of pulling my foot out as well, I hook it around the inside of Einstein's left hip. This puts Einstein in my butterfly guard.

As Einstein sits back to reestablish his base, I sit up with him. Keeping my over-hook tight, I secure an under-hook with my right arm. This puts me in the Cocoon and opens all sorts of attacks.

The Jailbreak (arm hook)

A lot of opponents won't attempt to pin you to the mat with head and arm control when they reach side control. Instead, they will keep one hand wrapped around your head and hook their other arm around your leg. It's more of a traditional Brazilian Jiu-Jitsu side control, and its main goal is too keep your from being able to turn into your opponent. You can still perform the Jailbreak when an opponent claims this position, but instead of establishing a butterfly hook on the inside of his thigh, you are going to hook the inside of his arm. Be forewarned, this requires a lot of flexibility.

Einstein is in side control, pinning my shoulders to the mat using his head and arm control.

Einstein releases his head and arm control. He scoops his right arm underneath my right leg to prevent me from turning into him. As he does this, I elevate my right leg to hinder him from climbing into the mount position.

I grab my left foot with my left hand and pull it towards my head.

With the aid of my left hand, I hook my foot underneath Einstein's right armpit. To keep Einstein from spinning into the North/South position, I continue to drive my right hand into his left hip.

I use my left hook to lift Einstein's body away from me. This gives me room to slip my right knee underneath my left leg and spin my hips into Einstein.

I hook my right foot around the inside of Einstein's left hip.

I drop my left foot and hook it around the inside of Einstein's right hip, putting him in my butterfly guard. As he sits back to reestablish his base, I follow him up and secure an under-hook with my right arm. This puts me in the Cocoon.

MASTERING THE RUBBER GUARD

The Tunnel

This move is a little trickier than some of the other escapes. First off, it requires more flexibility because you're going to establish your first butterfly hook without the use of your hands. You also have to mask your intentions. If your opponent senses that you are going for the Jailbreak, he will transition into Judo Side Control by dropping down to his side. If he does this, the space you need to execute this technique, as well as the other Jailbreaks, will be severed. Judo Side Control kills all Jailbreaks. In order to pull off the technique, you want to really drive your knee up into your opponent's side. Your opponent will most likely take your overexaggeration as a desperate maneuver to avoid the mount. But in reality you are only trying to get his mind off the Jailbreak and create the space needed to execute the technique.

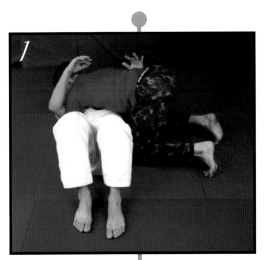

Einstein is in side control, pinning my shoulders to the mat using his head and arm control.

Securing a tight over-hook with my right arm, I push off the mat with my right foot, elevate my hips, and dig my left knee into Einstein's ribs. He interprets my action as a desperate attempt to avoid the mount, which takes his focus off the options available to me. Remember, the moment your opponent senses something funny, he will probably drop into Judo Side Control to avoid all your Jailbreak options.

Before Einstein can drop his hips back down on top of me, I swing my right leg behind my left and dig my foot to the inside of his left hip.

Using my right butterfly hook, I lift Einstein's body off me. I use the created space to spin my hips into him, slide my left knee underneath his body, and hook my left foot around the outside of his left hip.

Continuing to spin into Einstein, I drop my left foot down to the inside of his right hip. I also hook my left arm underneath his right arm to secure an under-hook.

As Einstein sits back to reestablish is base, I sit up with him. To maintain the Cocoon position, I lock my under-hook and over-hook down tight.